PLANNING LAW

Law Essentials

PLANNING LAW

Anne-Michelle Slater,
B.A.(Dub), M.R.T.P.I.(UCD)

*Senior Lecturer in Law,
University of Aberdeen*

DUNDEE UNIVERSITY PRESS
2010

First edition published in Great Britain in 2010 by
Dundee University Press
University of Dundee
Dundee DD1 4HN

www.dundee.ac.uk/dup

ISBN 978 1 84586 110 0

No natural forests were destroyed to make this product; only farmed timber was used
and replanted.

British Library Cataloguing-in-Publication Data
A catalogue record for this book is available on request from the British Library

Typeset by Waverley Typesetters, Warham, Norfolk
Printed and bound by Bell & Bain Ltd, Glasgow

CONTENTS

TABLE OF CASES

TABLE OF STATUTES

1 INTRODUCTION

"We want our planning system to return to the vision of Patrick Geddes, the Scot who is the father of town planning who saw the need for a system that balanced the needs of 'folk, work and place', but with a fourth objective – fairness" (Foreword to the Scottish Executive White Paper, *Modernising the Planning System* (2005)).

"I feel sorry for J K Rowling that her creation of Hogwarts really can't match the magnificent complexities of our new planning system" (Neil Collar, Brodies Planning Blog).

The new planning system has now largely been implemented. It has, however, been a very long time coming and it is still not clear whether it achieves its original aspirations, as set out in the first quote above. The process of reform commenced even before the start of devolution, with the publication of *Land Use Planning under a Scottish Parliament* (Scottish Executive, 1999), which indicated a willingness to consider major changes to the system, if they were shown to be necessary. There then followed an extensive process of consultation, which culminated in the Planning etc (Scotland) Bill. Introducing it to the Scottish Parliament, the Communities Minister described it as "the most fundamental and comprehensive reform of the planning system" since its creation in 1948. Key themes from the White Paper were translated into legislative proposals on the following:

- the role of the development plan;
- making the planning system fit for purpose;
- encouraging greater efficiency in the process;
- making it easier for people to become involved;
- recognising planning's role in delivering sustainable development.

The Bill received Royal Assent on 20 December 2006. This, however, was not the end of the process. The Planning etc (Scotland) Act 2006 (the "2006 Act") laid down a framework for change, based on the White Paper. The detail, however, has been delivered through extensive use of secondary legislation, which itself was subject to consultation and, in some cases, to affirmative procedure. The commencement timetable suffered severely from slippage and those involved in the process suffered from consultation fatigue. The starting gun for the new system, however, was fired at last, with the publication of *Delivering Planning Reform* (Scottish Government, 2008), with most of the main provisions of the 2006 Act being implemented by 3 August 2009. The process has been by amendment to the Town and Country Planning (Scotland) Act 1997 (the "1997 Act"), notwithstanding an early commitment, which subsequently lapsed, to provide a consolidated Act.

There are three elements which contribute to "the magnificent complexities of our new planning system". First, and most important, is the actual extent and nature of the reforms: planning law and practice in Scotland has fundamentally and comprehensively changed and will change further as the new development plans are completed. Second, is the level of amendment to the principal Act, which, even prior to 2006, had been incrementally amended since 1997. Third, is the extent of secondary legislation and planning circulars that accompany the amendments to the 1997 Act.

This text aims to explain the important changes to planning law in the context of the existing regime and therefore provide the *Essentials* of planning law in Scotland. It explains planning law as a whole, but with a focus on the recent reforms. In referring to these, the term "the 2006 Act reforms" is used and the relevant section in the amended 1997 Act noted.

This book does not cover listed building and conservation area legislation. Reform of this area is anticipated in the near future. It also does not deal in any detail with unreformed (and relatively underused) aspects of the planning system which are covered in the existing standard text books. Neither does it deal with areas of law that are related to planning law, such as building standards or roads legislation. There are still some important aspects of the Scottish planning law reform package which remain unimplemented and these areas have been highlighted in the text.

The law is stated as at 28 May 2010.

Essential Facts

- The principal planning Act is the Town and Country Planning (Scotland) Act 1997.
- Reform of the planning system in Scotland was the subject of extensive debate and consultation by the Scottish Executive between 1999 and 2004.

- A White Paper, *Modernising the Planning System*, was published in 2005.
- Planning reform legislation was provided by the Planning etc (Scotland) Act 2006 which generally amends the principal Act (2006 Act reforms).
- The reform process has also been achieved through secondary legislation.
- Most of the new system was implemented by 3 August 2009.

2 ORGANISATION AND ADMINISTRATION OF PLANNING IN SCOTLAND

Land use planning in Scotland is primarily a local and national park authority function (*Scottish Planning Policy* (2010), para 8). Central government, however, monitors, co-ordinates and to a large extent controls this. This chapter sets out the roles and responsibilities of Scottish Ministers, planning authorities, key agencies and some of the other important organisations and bodies involved in the planning system in Scotland.

SCOTTISH MINISTERS AND THE SCOTTISH EXECUTIVE/GOVERNMENT

The devolved powers of the Scottish Parliament extend to town and country planning legislation and include laws on compulsory purchase. Many other functions which impinge on planning are also part of the devolution settlement, including environment, agriculture, forestry and fishing; economic development and transport; local government, social work and housing; sport and the arts. Following the 2007 elections to the Scottish Parliament, a minority administration was formed by the Scottish National Party, which is committed to full independence for Scotland. Its central and overarching purpose is to focus the government and public services on creating a more successful country, with opportunities for all of Scotland to flourish, through increasing sustainable economic growth (*Scottish Government Economic Strategy* (2007), p vii). It has five strategic objectives for Scotland to become: wealthier and fairer; greener; smarter; safer; and stronger and healthier. This is reflected in all their policy documents, including those relating to planning. One presentational symbolic change, rapidly introduced, was to rebrand the Scottish Executive as the Scottish Government (C Warren, *Managing Scotland's Environment* (2nd edn, 2009), p 32). They also completely reorganised the government's administrative structure. Six Cabinet Secretaries were appointed, with planning coming under the Finance and Sustainable Growth portfolio and currently the responsibility of the Cabinet Secretary for Finance and Sustainable Growth. There are two Ministers, with the Minister for Transport, Infrastructure and Climate Change being the lead one for most planning issues.

Scottish Ministers 2007–11

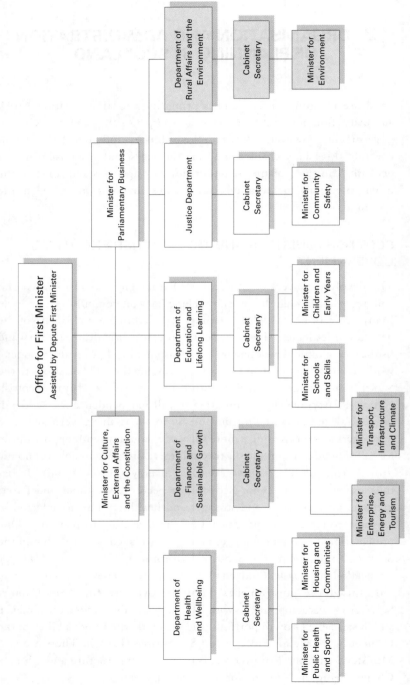

The Scottish Government's Directorate of the Built Environment

The Scottish Government's Directorate of the Built Environment is responsible for issues relating to planning matters at national level in Scotland. It consists of four divisions:

(1) Planning Legislation Performance, Sustainable Growth, Engagement and Strategic Environmental Assessment;
(2) Architecture and Place;
(3) National Spatial Planning, Aquaculture and North;
(4) Planning Reform, ePlanning and South.

Directorate for Planning and Environmental Appeals

The Directorate for Planning and Environmental Appeals is responsible for the administration of the Planning Appeals system. Its reporters deal with planning and related appeals. They take decisions on 99 per cent of appeals (known as delegated appeals) and prepare and submit reports with a recommendation to Scottish Ministers on "non-delegated" or recalled planning appeals. The appeals decided by Scottish Ministers raise issues of national importance.

Other divisions within the Scottish Government also relate, in some way, to planning, land use and the environment, but are not included in this text.

SCOTTISH MINISTERS

Scottish Ministers have a number of important powers, functions and duties relating to planning. The 2006 Act reforms have changed the nature and extent of the role of Scottish Ministers in the planning process in Scotland. These planning powers and responsibilities are now itemised under the general headings of: the National Planning Framework; Planning Applications; and Development Plan Functions.

The National Planning Framework

Scottish Ministers are required to prepare and publish the National Planning Framework (1997 Act, s 3A(6)(a)). (See Chapter 3 of this book for more detail.)

Planning applications

The powers of Scottish Ministers relating to planning applications are considered under three headings of:

- call-in;
- hierarchy of developments;
- delegation agreements.

Notifications and call-in

Scottish Ministers have a general power to intervene by calling in any application for planning permission for their own determination by way of a Direction (1997 Act, s 46(1)). This may be given either to a particular planning authority or to planning authorities generally and may relate either to a particular application or to applications of a class specified in the Direction (1997 Act, s 46(2)(a) and (b)). The changes to the processes and requirements for notifying Scottish Ministers are set out in Planning Circular 3/2009: *Notification of Planning Applications* and the Town and Country Planning (Notification of Applications) (Scotland) Direction 2009. It is considered that the revised system for national involvement in planning cases "... retains an appropriate level of national security in circumstances where the Scottish Government should rightly be involved, but removes from the notification process the vast majority of applications which raise no issues of national interest" (Planning Circular 3/2009: *Notification of Planning Applications*, para 10). (See Chapter 7 of this book for more details.)

These are as follows:

(1) Development in which planning authorities have an interest:
   (a) for which the planning authority is the applicant or developer;
   (b) in respect of which the planning authority has a financial or other interest; or
   (c) is to be located on land which is wholly or partly in the planning authority's ownership or in which it has an interest.

(2) Objection by Government Agency relating to:
   (a) development affecting trunk road and special roads;
   (b) development in the vicinity of major hazards;
   (c) nature conservation;
   (d) scheduled monuments and category A listed buildings;
   (e) flooding;
   (f) playing fields;
   (g) marine fish farm developments;

(3) Open cast coal and related minerals.

There are tolerances for (a)–(g) set out in the Schedule to the Direction. This list represents a reduction in the types of application that require to be notified to Scottish Ministers. The revised system is designed to be more proportionate and to apply only to applications which raise issues of national importance (Planning Circular 3/2009: *Notification of Applications*, para 8). In relation to other categories of development, the Scottish Ministers will issue case-specific notification directions to require specific applications to be notified to Scottish Ministers. This will be done only where it appears that there is some matter of national interest involved which requires consideration by Scottish Ministers.

The information to be sent to Scottish Ministers is set out in the 2009 Direction. The effect of notification to Scottish Ministers of intention by a planning authority to approve an application is that it effectively puts a brake on the approval process. The planning authority must not approve the application until 28 days has expired from the date of receipt by Scottish Ministers of all the relevant information on the notified planning application. The Scottish Ministers, within that 28-day period, decide whether to call in the application for their own determination (1997 Act, s 46). Where it takes longer to reach a decision as to whether the application should be called in, Scottish Ministers will issue a further direction to extend their period of consultation. If at the end of the 28-day period, or any extended period, the Scottish Government has not issued a direction or extended the period for consideration, the planning authority can proceed to determine the application (Circular 3/2009, para 28).

Hierarchy of developments

The 2006 Act reforms introduced the concept of a hierarchy of developments consisting of "national developments" (1997 Act, s 3A(4)(b)), "major developments" and "local developments" (1997 Act, s 26(2)). Scottish Ministers identify the classes of development, other than national developments, and assign each class to one or other of the categories (Town and Country Planning (Hierarchy of Developments) (Scotland) Regulations 2009 and Planning Circular 5/2009: *Hierarchy of Developments*).

Schemes of delegation

The 2006 Act reforms introduced a new additional scheme of delegation for local developments "to support an efficient planning process" (1997 Act, s 43A). All planning authorities are required to have delegation agreements for local developments (Town and Country Planning (Schemes of Delegation and Local Review Procedure) (Scotland) Regulations 2008). It is, however, for each planning authority to determine the level of delegation to officers. Planning Circular 7/2009: *Scheme of Delegation and Local Reviews*, advises that Scottish Ministers wish to encourage planning authorities to make the most effective use of their powers by delegating decision-making on straightforward planning applications to officers. Scottish Ministers must approve the delegation agreements prior to adoption by planning authorities.

Development Plan functions

Scottish Ministers are involved in the development plan process in a number of ways. The most important is the approval of Strategic Development Plans and the adoption of Local Development Plans. These and the other aspects of development planning and Scottish Ministers' functions are described under the following headings:

- Designation of Strategic Development Plan Areas;
- Development Plan Schemes;
- Strategic Development Plans;
- Local Development Plans;
- Action programmes;
- Supplementary guidance.

Designation of Strategic Development Plan Areas

One of the first manifestations of the 2006 Act reforms was the designation by Scottish Ministers of groups of planning authorities, as strategic development planning authorities (SDPAs) to prepare and review strategic development plans (SDPs) (1997 Act, s 4(1)). These plans replace structure plans in Scotland and form part of the development plan. The next stage in the reform process was the determination of the boundary of each SDPA by Scottish Ministers. Three months after their designation, SDPAs were required to submit a plan showing a proposed boundary to Scottish Ministers, with a justification for their proposal (1997 Act, s 5(1)). Scottish Ministers determine the boundary of the Strategic Development Plan Area:

- as proposed in the submission;
- the proposed boundary with such modifications as they think fit; or
- such other boundary as they think fit (1997 Act, s 5(3)).

The current SDPA Designation Orders came into force on 25 June 2008, designating four areas centred on the cities of Edinburgh, Glasgow, Aberdeen and Dundee (Planning Circular 3/2008: *Strategic Development Plan Areas*).

Development Plan Schemes

Each planning authority and SDPA must prepare, at least once a year, a development plan scheme to set out the authority's programme for preparing and reviewing their SDP or Local Development Plan (LDP) (1997 Act, s 20B). It does not require approval from Scottish Ministers, but two copies must be sent to Scottish Ministers once adopted.

Strategic Development Plans (SDPs)

SDPAs are required by s 4(1) of the 1997 Act to prepare and review SDPs and submit these to Scottish Ministers within 4 years of the approval of the existing plan. There are a number of stages where Scottish Ministers are involved in the preparation process of the SDP. In preparing the main issues report, SDPAs are required to consult with and have regard to the views of Scottish Ministers. The proposed plan also has extensive consultation requirements, including with Scottish Ministers. The main role of Scottish Ministers, however, is in the approval process.

The SDPA is required to submit the SDP to Scottish Ministers, who will then appoint a person to examine the SDP where there are unresolved representations, where the proposed plan contains alternative proposals, or where Scottish Ministers otherwise consider an examination to be appropriate (2006 Act, s 12(1)). Scottish Ministers may approve the plan in whole or in part, modify it or reject it (1997 Act, s 13).

Local Development Plans

All planning authorities are required to prepare one or more local development plan (LDPs) for their area and, as with SDPs, Scottish Ministers are involved at various stages of the preparation process. This includes consultation on the main issues report and the proposed LDP. The most important stage is the requirement for submission of the plan to Scottish Ministers. An examination of the plan may be undertaken and the subsequent recommendations are largely binding on planning authorities (Town and Country Planning (Grounds for declining to follow recommendations) (Scotland) Regulations 2009, reg 2). There are detailed procedures relating to adoption of the LDP, including modifications to the plan required by Scottish Ministers.

Action programmes

Action programmes will set out how the new suite of development plans will be implemented. The authorities are to consult and consider the views of, *inter alia,* Scottish Ministers. The proposed action programmes must be published and submitted to Scottish Ministers alongside proposed SDPs and LDPs. They must be adopted and published within 3 months of the plan, to which it relates, being approved/adopted.

Supplementary guidance

The 2006 Act reforms allow much detailed material, previously contained within local plans, to be provided by supplementary guidance, allowing the plans themselves to focus on vision, the spatial strategy, overarching and other key policies and proposals. There are certain requirements relating to the role of Scottish Ministers and the creation of supplementary guidance. Primarily, Scottish Ministers will scrutinise the guidance before it can be adopted by planning authorities. It is anticipated, however, that this pre-adoption scrutiny will focus more on ensuring that the principles of good public involvement and a proper connection with the SDP or LDP have been achieved consistently, than on detailed policy content. Nevertheless, the proposed supplementary guidance must be submitted to Scottish Ministers and a period of 28 days must elapse before the supplementary guidance is adopted and issued (1997 Act, s 22(6)). At any time before the supplementary guidance is adopted, Scottish Ministers may require a planning authority to make modifications or direct the authority not to adopt and issue it.

Comment on the role of Scottish Ministers in the planning system

Planning has always been a local process in Scotland, notwithstanding that central government monitors, co-ordinates and often controls it. The Scottish Government has signalled that it will scale back the level of centralised planning advice to allow local solutions to be developed. However, Rowan Robinson has observed that "the reforms seem likely to result in some shift in power from planning authorities to the Executive" (*The Town and Country Planning (Scotland) Act 1997* (Green's Annotated Acts, 2009), p viii). It may be, therefore, that Scottish Ministers have less involvement in the day-to-day operation of the local planning administration but an increased controlling and co-ordinating role on the larger, strategically important developments. Getting this balance right will be an early test of the new planning regime in Scotland.

PLANNING AUTHORITIES

The primary responsibility for the operation of the planning system and service is with local and national park authorities (*Scottish Planning Policy* (2008), para 8). Since 1996 there have been 29 single-tier or unitary local authorities and three island authorities in Scotland (Local Government etc (Scotland) Act 1994). Each local authority is the planning authority for its area (1997 Act, s 1(1)), except where one of Scotland's two national parks is located within its district (National Parks (Scotland) Act 2000). There are four strategic planning authorities where there is joint working of more than one local authority to produce the Strategic Development Plan.

The main powers of the local planning authority, as set out in the Town and Country Planning (Scotland) Act 1997, as amended by the Planning etc (Scotland) Act 2006 and the National Parks (Scotland) Act 2000, are as follows:

(1) preparation of the development plans, which should contribute to sustainable development;

(2) implementation, monitoring and review of plans;

(3) formation of supplementary planning guidance;

(4) development management, including: pre-application discussion; decisions on submission of an environmental assessment; determination of planning applications and revocation or modification of an existing consent;

(5) enforcement of planning control;

(6) tree protection;

(7) advertisement control (including fly posting);

(8) acquisition of land for planning purposes;

(9) control and review of mineral workings and planning permissions for mineral operations, including revocation or suspension of permission;

(10) ability to enter into planning agreements obligations with land owners and developers.

Most of these activities are dealt with in this book.

Local authorities have extensive powers including, *inter alia*, under the Planning (Listed Buildings and Conservation Areas) (Scotland) Act 1997, the advertising legislation, and the hazardous substances laws. These topics are not covered in this text.

Most planning authority functions relate to the local authority area in which they are located and planning jurisdiction was restricted to the area above the low-water mark of tidal waters (*Argyll and Bute District Council v Secretary of State for Scotland* (1976)). There are three exceptions to this: strategic development plan areas, aquaculture and national parks.

STRATEGIC DEVELOPMENT PLAN AREAS

The SDPAs are as follows:

Glasgow and the Clyde Valley Strategic Development Plan Area

The Glasgow and the Clyde Valley Strategic Development Plan Area constitutes the administrative areas of East Dunbartonshire, East Renfrewshire, Glasgow City, Inverclyde, North Lanarkshire, Renfrewshire, South Lanarkshire and West Dunbartonshire Councils, excepting the part of West Dunbartonshire Council that formed part of the Loch Lomond and the Trossachs National Park on 11 November 2008.

Aberdeen City and Shire Strategic Development Plan Area

The Aberdeen City and Shire Strategic Development Plan Area constitutes the administrative areas of Aberdeen City and Aberdeenshire Councils, excepting the part of Aberdeenshire Council that formed part of the Cairngorms National Park on 11 November 2008.

Dundee, Perth, Angus and North Fife Strategic Development Plan Area

The Dundee, Perth, Angus and North Fife Strategic Development Plan Area constitutes the administrative areas of Angus, Dundee City and Perth and Kinross Councils and part of Fife Council, excepting the part of Angus Council that formed part of the Cairngorms National Park and the part of Perth and Kinross Council that formed part of the Loch Lomond and the Trossachs National Park on 11 November 2008. The boundary for the Cairngorms National Park is being extended south in October 2010. This will reduce the area of the SDPA, as it will then be excluded from the plan area (see "Changes to national parks in Scotland", below, for more details).

Edinburgh and South East Scotland Strategic Development Plan Area

The Edinburgh and South East Scotland Strategic Development Plan Area constitutes the administrative areas of City of Edinburgh, East Lothian,

Midlothian, Scottish Borders and West Lothian Councils and that part of Fife Council illustrated on Map 3 of Planning Circular 3/2008: *Strategic Development Plan Areas*.

AQUACULTURE

The extension of planning controls to marine fish farming was included in the 2006 Act reforms (1997 Act, ss 26(1) and (6) and 26AA), although the principle had been enshrined in the Water Environment and Water Services (Scotland) Act 2003. The effect is that all new fish farms, or modifications to existing ones, require planning permission from the appropriate local authority. Marine planning zones have been created, with each designated as the planning authority for the purposes of aquaculture within a particular zone (Town and Country Planning (Marine Fish Farming) (Scotland) Order 2007, art 5). Aquaculture, however, will increasingly become part of the new marine planning regime introduced by the Marine (Scotland) Act 2010. To this end, an Aquaculture Planning Taskforce prepared *Delivering Planning Reform for Aquaculture* (March 2010).

NATIONAL PARKS

The creation of national parks for Scotland is recognised as one of the achievements of the first Scottish Parliament, although the process leading to their establishment has been described as long and tortuous (Warren, *Managing Scotland's Environment*, p 237). The National Parks (Scotland) Act 2000 (the "2000 Act") is enabling legislation which sets a framework for all future national parks in Scotland. In particular, it confers on Scottish Ministers the power to propose an area for designation as a National Park, with a corresponding National Park Authority to exercise certain functions. Scotland now has two national parks: the Loch Lomond and the Trossachs National Park and the Cairngorms National Park. Their creation has been regarded as an expression of the post-devolution nation-building agenda, which sought to demonstrate the added value and distinctive approach of the Scottish Parliament (A Rennie, "The Importance of National Parks to Nation Building: Support for the National Park Act (2000) in the Scottish Parliament" (2006) 122(3) *Scottish Geographical Journal* 223 as quoted in Warren, *Managing Scotland's Environment*, p 237). The "Scottish national park legislation reflects wider environmental concerns [and] ... a strong local voice in the running of the parks" (C T Reid, *Nature Conservation* (3rd edn, 2009), para 5.9.24).

Designation of a national park

In order to qualify for national park status an area must satisfy three criteria (2000 Act, s 2(2)):

- it must be of outstanding and national importance for its natural and/or cultural heritage;
- it should have a distinctive character and a coherent identity; and
- creating a national park should be the best means of meeting the particular needs of the area.

Proposals for a national park are made to Scottish Ministers and followed by a report by SNH (or another public body appointed for this purpose) considering the desirability of the designation, the area to be designated, the functions for the park authority, the costs involved and any other specified matters. Preparation of this report must involve consultation with local authorities, community councils, and representatives of those who live, work or carry on business in the area, and must take into account the views expressed (2000 Act, s 3). The final stage is for Scottish Ministers to make a designation order, which must have regard to the report. The order must be approved in draft by the Scottish Parliament, after a further extensive consultation exercise. The draft may be revised in light of the responses. The Parliament is informed of the views received during consultation and any changes being made at this stage (2000 Act, s 6). The final designation order is then made by statutory instrument.

Aims of a national park

The aims of the national park are set out in s 1 of the 2000 Act:

(a) to conserve and enhance the natural and cultural heritage of the area;

(b) to promote sustainable use of the natural resources of the area;

(c) to promote understanding and enjoyment (including enjoyment in the form of recreation) of the special qualities of the area by the public; and

(d) to promote sustainable economic and social development of the area's communities.

The general purpose of the Park Authorities is to ensure that these aims are collectively achieved in a co-ordinated way in relation to each park (2000 Act, s 9). In the event of any conflict between these aims, greater weight must be given to the first aim. Reid observes that the detailed administrative arrangements for and the precise powers of each National Park Authority are determined on an individual basis for each park, with the framework being established by the Act (*Nature Conservation*, paras 5.9.28–5.9.37).

Planning functions of national parks

The arrangements for the exercise of planning functions in a national park are specified in the designation order which establishes it.

These may take the form of the following:

- the National Park Authority being the planning authority for the area of the park;
- the National Park Authority being the planning authority only in respect of development plan preparation;
- the National Park Authority having such functions in respect of planning as the designation order specifies.

The Loch Lomond and the Trossachs National Park Designation, Transitional and Consequential Provisions (Scotland) Order 2002 designated Loch Lomond and the Trossachs as the first National Park in Scotland. It was established on 8 July 2002 as a National Park Authority for the designated area. The Loch Lomond and the Trossachs Park Authority has full planning powers within its area; it therefore determines all planning applications and has the power to take enforcement action.

The Cairngorms National Park Designation, Transitional and Consequential Provisions (Scotland) Order 2003 designated the Cairngorms as the second National Park. The National Park Authority for the area was established on 25 March 2003. In the case of the Cairngorms, the planning powers of the Park Authority are limited to sole responsibility for preparing local development plans for the park area; it has shared responsibility with the relevant local authorities (Aberdeenshire, Angus, Highland and Moray Councils) for enforcement and special controls over trees, amenity notices and advertisements. Local authorities, in exercising their planning functions, are under an obligation to pay "special attention" to the desirability of exercising powers consistently with the park plan (1997 Act, s 264A). The Cairngorms Park Authority is a consultee on all planning applications within the National Park boundary. It has the power to call in for determination those planning applications which it considers raise issues of general significance for the statutory National Park aims.

National Park Plan

A National Park authority has a duty to prepare and submit to Scottish Ministers a National Park Plan. The plan sets out the authority's policy for managing the park and for co-ordinating the exercise of its functions and those of other public bodies in relation to the park. There is a clear statutory duty on Scottish Ministers, the Authority, local authorities and all other public bodies and office holders to have regard to the plan in the exercise of their functions, so far as they affect the park (2006 Act, s 14). In reporting on the Cairngorm National Park Local Plan, clarification was provided on the status of the National Park Plan, as the most important strategic planning document for the park (Local Plan Report, December 2009). Furthermore, "the effectiveness of the Park Plan will be crucial to the smooth working and success of the parks ... and in particular there is a clear need for the park plan and the development plans to be consistent" (Reid, *Nature Conservation*, para 5.9.33). At the time of writing, both national park authorities have a National Park Plan (2007–12) and are in the process of completing a local plan (a pre-2006 Act reforms development plan). In future it is anticipated that the new LDP and the National Park Plan will be developed in tandem.

Changes to national parks in Scotland

A number of changes in relation to national parks are to be implemented. A proposal to extend the southern boundary of Cairngorm National Park to include part of Perth and Kinross was reported on by SNH in 2008 and laid before Parliament in 2009. This extension will be implemented in October 2010. In 2008, the Scottish Government conducted a strategic review of Scotland's National Park Authorities. One of the Review recommendations was for fewer members of the National Park Authority, to support consistently effective governance. The review recommendations were consulted upon and the Scottish Government published a report in August 2009. National Park Authority Board members will therefore be reduced from 25 to 19 in Cairngorms and to 17 in Loch Lomond and the Trossachs. The changes will be implemented by amendments to the Designation Orders, which, in relation to the Cairngorms National Park, will also enable the extension of the boundary. A strategy group on National Parks in Scotland chaired by the Minister for the Environment has also been established. It is expected that further national parks will be designated in Scotland in the coming years.

DECISION-MAKING IN PLANNING AUTHORITIES

The planning powers vested in local authorities are exercised by the elected representatives or councillors for each local authority area. Traditionally, decisions on planning matters took the form of a meeting of the full council or by the planning committee. There has always been an option to delegate decision-making powers on planning applications to an appointed officer, usually, the Director of Planning. Prior to the implementation of the 2006 Act reforms, most planning authorities in Scotland had a formal delegation agreement to cover at least minor or uncontroversial planning applications. Many had a much more extensive arrangement and only the most significant applications were determined by a committee. The Scottish Government's current expectation, through the reform of the planning system, is that schemes of delegation will provide maximum scope for officials to determine planning applications, thus ensuring elected members' focus on complex or controversial issues. The introduction of a hierarchy for development management radically alters the way in which decisions are made and in particular increases the amount of decision-making by officers. This, combined with an extension of permitted development rights, will reduce the number of planning applications to be determined by the planning authority.

KEY AGENCIES AND OTHER BODIES RELEVANT TO THE FUNCTION OF PLANNING

A wide range of bodies exercise functions and powers conferred by Acts of Parliament and other statutory provisions relating to planning in Scotland. The main functions are undertaken by local authorities, national parks and Scottish Government, but there are many other bodies involved to a greater or lesser extent. The reform process has identified key agencies involved in the planning process, which have particular statutory functions. This section considers the law and policy role of the key agencies. It also identifies the other bodies and sets out their functions and powers in relation to the planning process in Scotland.

Key agencies

The new planning regime has included the term "key agencies" within the legislation (1997 Act, s 23D). The Town and Country Planning (Development Planning) Regulations 2008 identify the key agencies and set out their duties and responsibilities:

Key government agencies

- Historic Scotland
- Scottish Environment Protection Agency (SEPA)
- Scottish Natural Heritage (SNH)

Other key agencies

- Architecture and Design Scotland (A+DS)
- Scottish Water
- Transport Scotland

Key agencies in appropriate locations

- Scottish Enterprise
- Highlands and Islands Enterprise (HIE)
- The Crofters Commission
- Regional Transport Partnerships
- Regional Health Boards.

The key agencies have made a number of commitments in relation to the planning process – for example, not to comment on development proposals, unless doing so adds real value to the process, and, to endeavour to ensure that their responses are given within agreed timescales (Scottish Government Planning Reform – Key Agencies' Contribution, Spring Road Shows, 2009). A uniformity of approach and a commitment to the planning process was jointly set out in the Scottish Government Spring Road Shows, 2009, as follows:

> "We, the Key Government Agencies (Historic Scotland, SEPA and SNH), are fully aligned to the Government's Economic Strategy and the delivery of sustainable growth. We rely on the planning system to achieve the outcomes sought by the Government and the delivery of the Government's Economic Strategy on the ground. We have a critical role in protecting and safeguarding the integrity of the natural and built environment whilst enabling 'good development to happen in the right places'. We will offer our expertise, make our advice as clear and consistent as possible, speed up our response times, and improve our internal performance and improve our communications and stakeholders advice and work alongside stakeholders in the planning system to enable development that is sustainable."

The roles and responsibilities of each key agency in Scotland are now considered. They are set out in alphabetical order.

Architecture and Design Scotland (A+DS)

A+DS, established in 2005, is an advisory Non-Departmental Public Body (NDPB). It operates as a company limited by guarantee funded directly by the Scottish Government. Its role is to deliver the Scottish Ministers' design and architecture policies and to inspire better quality in design and architecture. Its responsibilities include providing support through design review.

Crofters Commission

The Crofters Commission was established in 1955, to serve the interests of the crofting community throughout the highlands of Scotland (s 1 of the Crofters (Scotland) Act 1955, now s 1 of the Crofters (Scotland) Act 1993). It operates as an NDPB of the Scottish Government Rural Affairs Directorate and is identified as a "key agency" for the purposes of development planning where strategic or local development plans relate to crofting counties.

Historic Scotland

Historic Scotland is an established executive agency of the Scottish Government. It is charged with protecting historic buildings, parks, gardens and landscapes, ancient monuments and archaeological sites and promoting public understanding and enjoyment of the man-made heritage in Scotland. It exercises statutory functions under the Ancient Monuments and Archaeological Areas Act 1979 and the Planning (Listed Buildings and Conservation Areas) (Scotland) Act 1997. Its planning functions include advising Scottish Ministers on scheduling monuments of national importance, listing buildings of special architectural or historic interest, listing historic wrecks and responding to consultations on applications (see *A Joint Working Agreement Between Historic Scotland and Planning Authorities in Relation to Statutory Casework and Consultation* (2008)).

Scottish Enterprise and Highlands and Islands Enterprise

Scottish Enterprise (SE) and Highlands and Islands Enterprise (HIE) were established by the Enterprise and New Towns (Scotland) Act 1990. Scottish Enterprise is Scotland's main economic, enterprise, innovation and investment agency. Together with HIE, it promotes economic development and training through a network of Local Enterprise Companies (LECs). They are key agencies only where the SDP or LDP in question relates to an area within which or in relation to which SE or HIE have statutory functions (Town and Country Planning (Development Planning) (Scotland) Regulations 2008, reg 28(2) and (3)).

Scottish Environment Protection Agency

The Scottish Environment Protection Agency (SEPA) was established as an NDPB by s 20(1) of the Environment Act 1995 and is the environmental regulator for Scotland. The key agency role for SEPA is to protect and improve the environment through its regulatory process. It is a statutory consultee on planning applications where development has an environmental aspect, including flooding, waste, drainage and pollution. Development plans should be prepared in line with advice given by SEPA: for example, strategic drainage issues (Scottish Executive, Development Department, Planning Advice Note 79: *Water and Drainage* (2006), para 23). SEPA must also provide information to those preparing Environmental Statements and advise local planning authorities on the content of those statements (Scottish Executive, Development Department, Planning Advice Note 51: *Planning and Environmental Protection*, para 60 (produced in connection with the Environment and Rural Affairs Department and SEPA) (2006)).

Scottish Natural Heritage

Scottish Natural Heritage (SNH) was established in 1992 by the Natural Heritage (Scotland) Act 1991. It is a government body and is accountable to Scottish Ministers and the Scottish Parliament. It must secure the conservation and enhancement of Scotland's natural heritage, help people to enjoy and value it, and encourage people to use it sustainably. SNH is a statutory consultee, under the Town and Country Planning (Development Management) (Scotland) Regulations 2008, in cases where development proposals may affect an area of special interest notified to the planning authority by SNH or where the development consists of or includes the commercial winning and working of peat. SNH also has duties under other legislation, related to land use planning, including the Wildlife and Countryside Act 1981, the Land Reform (Scotland) Act 2003 and the Nature Conservation (Scotland) Act 2004.

Scottish Water

Scottish Water was established by s 20 of and Sch 3 to the Water Industry (Scotland) Act 2002 and is publicly owned and answerable to the Scottish Parliament. It is responsible for the public water and drainage system and has a statutory duty to contribute to the achievement of sustainable development in carrying out its operations (Scottish Government, Planning Advice Note 61: *Planning and Sustainable Water Drainage Systems* (2001), para 21).

Scottish Water is responsible for co-ordinating and delivering invest-ment in its water and waste-water infrastructure and grants consent for connection to its network. It takes into consideration the views and development priorities expressed by the local authority in its development plan and advises the planning authority on the current and programmed capability to accommodate development. Planning authorities are expected to consult Scottish Water when preparing drainage area plans and it will also have pre-application discussions with developers to identify capacity for development and the options if the existing network is incapable of meeting the needs of development proposals. Scottish Water is a statutory consultee on applications involving proposals which are likely to require material additions to or changes in the services it provides. As a "key agency" in the planning system, it is expected to maintain, protect and deliver key infrastructure.

Transport Scotland

Transport Scotland is the national transport agency for Scotland. It was established in 2006 and its purpose is to help deliver the Scottish Government's vision for transport, using the national rail and road networks. Transport Scotland is regarded by Scottish Ministers as a key agency with a delivery function to maintain, protect and deliver the key infrastructure necessary for economic growth and development (Agency Roles, Scottish Government Planning Reform – Key Agencies' Contribution, Spring Road Shows, 2009). It should enable major infrastructure projects and deliver improvements to Scottish transport and infrastructure.

Regional transport partnerships and health boards

A regional transport partnership is specified as a key agency only where the strategic development plan or local development plan in question relates to the area of that transport partnership. A regional health board is specified as a key agency only where the strategic development plan or local development plan in question relates to the area of that health board.

Other relevant bodies and organisations

There are numerous other public and private bodies and organisations involved in the planning process in Scotland to a greater or lesser extent. In relation to the operation of the planning system in Scotland, the principal ones are: community councils, the Crown Estate, the Forestry Commission, the Health and Safety Executive, local authority and registered social landlords, district salmon boards, Network Rail, Sports

Scotland and Visit Scotland. Only community councils are explained in this text.

Community councils

Community councils were created by the Local Government etc (Scotland) Act 1973 and their functions involve ascertaining, co-ordinating and expressing the views of the local community to local authorities and other public bodies within their area (Local Government etc (Scotland) Act 1973, s 51(2)). They are regarded as key stakeholders in the planning system in Scotland because of their local knowledge and involvement with local authorities. There are about 1,200 community councils in Scotland (Planning Advice Note 47: *Community Councils and Planning* (1996), para 10). They receive weekly lists of planning applications made to the local planning authority or to Scottish Ministers which relate to land within their area (Town and Country Planning (Development Management Procedure) (Scotland) Regulations 2008, reg 23). They have a statutory right to consultation where the development is one which is likely to affect the amenity in the area of the community council. Consultation may be requested based on the weekly list within 7 working days of its issue by the local planning authority (Town and Country Planning (Development Management Procedure) (Scotland) Regulations 2008, reg 25 and Sch 5). Community Councils are also involved in the new pre-application process for national and major applications. (See Chapter 6.)The role of the community council focuses on monitoring the weekly lists, consulting with planning officers, holding meetings to gauge local opinion and making representations to the local planning department to express that opinion. The community council also comments and contributes at various stages in the development plan process.

The table below illustrates planning consultation in Scotland.

COMMENT ON THE ORGANISATION AND ADMINISTRATION OF PLANNING IN SCOTLAND

The process of organisation and administration of planning in Scotland grew and became more complicated and multi-layered in the 60 years after the introduction of the planning regime. However, the reforms to the planning system and resulting scrutiny afforded to the whole process, have imposed some rigour and refinements to the regime. In particular, the clarification of the role of the key agencies has been helpful. The whole procedure of implementing the planning reforms has meant that the organisations and people involved in the planning process in Scotland

Consultation: key agencies and statutory consultees

Body	Key agency	Statutory consultee
A+DS	✓	
Coal Authority		✓
Community council		✓
Crofters Commission	✓	
District salmon fisheries board		✓
HSE		✓
Historic Scotland	✓	✓
Network Rail		✓
Planning authorities		✓
Regional health boards	✓	
Regional transport partnerships	✓	
Roads authority		✓
SEPA	✓	✓
Scottish Ministers		✓
Scottish Water	✓	✓
SNH	✓	✓
The Theatres Trust		✓

have had to reorganise and reconsider their practices. However, the Scottish Ministers, in undertaking the reform of the planning system in Scotland were always clear that legislative change alone was insufficient to meet their policy objectives. The phrase "culture change" appeared a number of times in the White Paper, and is explained thus:

> "When we consider culture, we consider the complex set of relationships between those who operate the planning system, those who use it and those who are affected by the decisions which it takes. It is generally accepted that there is a need to improve the delivery of both development planning and development management services" (p 30).

It remains to be seen, however, whether this culture change in planning has been effective in Scotland.

Essential Facts

- Planning is primarily a local authority function.

The role of Scottish Ministers

- Scottish Ministers have an important role which has changed with the 2006 Act reforms.
- Scottish Ministers prepare the National Planning Framework (NPF).
- Scottish Ministers can call in certain planning applications for determination.

The role of Strategic Development Planning Authorities

- Groups of local planning authorities prepare Strategic Development Plans (SDP) (currently for Edinburgh, Glasgow, Aberdeen and Dundee).
- SDPs are sent to Scottish Ministers for approval.

The role of local planning authorities

- Local planning authorities prepare local development plans (LDPs).
- Scottish Ministers can order an examination of LDPs.
- Local planning authorities determine planning applications.
- Most planning applications determined under delegated powers.

The role of other bodies and organisations

- National Park Authorities have planning functions.
- Key agencies for the planning process have been identified.
- Many other bodies are involved in the planning process.

3 NATIONAL PLANNING POLICY

Planning law is characterised by the important role of policy and guidance at national and local level. This chapter covers the Scottish Government's planning policies which are contained within the following documents:

- National Planning Framework (2009);
- Scottish Planning Policy (2010);
- Designing Places (2001);
- Designing Streets (2010);
- Planning Circulars.

It also deals with Planning Advice Notes (PANs), which constitute good practice advice.

NATIONAL PLANNING FRAMEWORK

The National Planning Framework (NPF) is the Scottish Government's strategy for Scotland's long-term spatial development. The first NPF was published 1 April 2004, as a non-statutory document. It was a response to the *Review of Strategic Planning*, undertaken by the Scottish Executive in 2001. It was the first time Scotland as a whole was expressed in spatial terms and the document identified key issues and drivers for change, setting out a vision for Scotland to 2025. It was not intended to be a prescriptive blueprint, but was to be taken into consideration by planning authorities, in their development planning and development control functions, and by the Executive and other government agencies in policy and spending decisions. Rowan Robinson notes, however, that it stopped short of identifying any specific developments, development sites or expenditure commitments (*The Town and Country Planning (Scotland) Act 1997* (Green's Annotated Acts, 2009), p ix). The Scottish Parliament had no formal involvement in the development or adoption of the first NPF.

The 2006 Act reforms put the NPF on a statutory footing, by inserting a new Pt IA into the principal Act, taking effect from April 2007. Section 3A(1) of the 1997 Act states: "there is to be a spatial plan for Scotland to be known as the 'National Planning Framework'". It is to set out in broad terms how Scottish Ministers consider that the development and use of land "could and should" occur (1997 Act, s 3A(2)), by providing a Framework to contain a strategy for Scotland's spatial development and a statement of what Scottish Ministers consider to be the priorities for that development (1997 Act, s 3A(3)(a) and (b)).

National developments

The NPF can identify certain projects as "national developments". These are developments of national strategic importance (1997 Act, s 3A(4)(b)). There is, however, no definition of "national development", although the White Paper indicated that "major transport, water and drainage, energy and waste infrastructure projects, major areas of urban regeneration or expansion and large strategic business or industrial investments may fall within this category of development" (*Modernising the Planning System*, p 21). If the NPF designates a development as a national development, it must contain a statement by Scottish Ministers of their reasons for considering that there is a need for that development (1997 Act, s 3A(5)(a)). The statement must also contain statements as regards other matters pertaining to any designation of a national development (1997 Act, s 3A(5)(b)).

Developments designated as national developments will still require planning permission and other relevant consents, but Scottish Ministers may intervene at any stage of the process to ensure that decisions are made expeditiously. The subsequent consent process is, therefore, not concerned with the principle of the development, as identification as a national development in the NPF is considered to be the mechanism for establishing its need. The statements of need will be a "material consideration" in the determination of the planning applications for these developments. (See Chapter 7 below for more detail on the definition of a "material consideration".) Any subsequent examination of the detailed planning implications will only be concerned with matters such as siting, design and the mitigation of environmental impacts.

Preparation of the NPF

The NPF is to be prepared and published by Scottish Ministers (1997 Act, s 3A(6)(a) and (b)), with a review every 5 years from publication (1997 Act, s 3A(7)(a)). It must be preceded by a "participation statement", to include details of when and with whom consultation is likely to take place, its likely form and the steps to be taken to involve the public at large in the preparation or review (1997 Act, s 3A(10)). Scottish Ministers must subsequently supply to the Scottish Parliament a report on the extent to which the consultation actually undertaken conformed to the statement (1997 Act, s 3C(2)(a)).

The functions relating to the preparation of the NPF must be exercised with the objective of contributing to sustainable development (1997 Act, s 3D). This was introduced at a late stage in the passage of the Bill, in response to the Scottish Parliament Communities Committee report on Stage 1 of the Planning etc (Scotland) Bill. A similar requirement was included in the Bill from the outset for planning authorities exercising their development planning functions. In construing sustainable development, regard may be had to any guidance issued by Scottish Ministers (1997 Act, s 3E), now contained in *Scottish Planning Policy* (February 2010), paras 34–40.

The proposed NPF must be laid before the Scottish Parliament for a period of 60 days for parliamentary consideration (1997 Act, s 3B(1)). Scottish Ministers are not to complete the NPF until this period has expired. The final version will have regard to any resolution or report of, or any committee of, the Scottish Parliament, made during the period of parliamentary consideration (1997 Act, s 3B(3)). The final decision on the content of the NPF, however, rests with Scottish Ministers, as parliamentary approval is not required.

Status of the NPF

Section 25(1)(b) of the 1997 Act makes it clear that, while the NPF is not part of the development plan, any reference to a national development in the NPF will require that the related determinations will also have regard to the relevant parts of the NPF. Otherwise, the NPF stands as a "material consideration". Planning authorities are required to take the NPF into account in preparing development plans and in the event of incompatibility between the NPF and the development plan, which ever is later in date is to prevail (1997 Act, s 25(2)(b)).

Overview of NPF2

The preparation of NPF2 took over 2 years, from February 2007 to publication of the final version on 25 June 2009.

There were five stages in the process:

- February–October 2007: initial engagement on scope and content;
- January–April 2008: issue of NPF2 discussion draft;
- April–November 2008: revision in light of reaction to the discussion draft;
- December 2008–March 2009: consideration of the proposed NPF2 in Parliament;
- March–June 2009: final considerations and publication of NPF2.

NPF2 has been subject to strategic environmental assessment (the Environmental Assessment (Scotland) Act 2005) and a strategic level appropriate assessment in relation to the integrity of Natura 2000 sites, Special Areas for Conservation, and Special Protection Areas. Ramsar Sites were also taken into account.

NPF2 describes Scotland in 2008/09. It identifies key issues and drivers of change and sets out a vision for Scotland to 2030, as a spatial representation of the Scottish Government's policy. It is closely linked to the Scottish Government's Infrastructure Investment Plan and identifies strategic priorities for investment in transport links, energy infrastructure, water and drainage capacity and waste management facilities.

National Developments NPF2

NPF2 identifies 14 national developments for 2009–30 as follows:

- Replacement Forth Crossing;
- West of Scotland Strategic Rail Enhancements;
- High Speed Rail Link to London;
- Strategic Airport Enhancements (for access);
- Grangemouth Freight Hub;
- Additional Container Freight Capacity on the Forth;
- Port developments on Loch Ryan;
- Scapa Flow Container Transhipment Facility;
- New Power Station and Transhipment Hub at Hunterston;
- New Non-Nuclear Baseload Capacity at other existing Power Station Sites;
- Electricity Grid Reinforcements;
- Central Scotland Green Network;
- Metropolitan Glasgow Strategic Drainage Scheme;
- 2014 Commonwealth Games Facilities.

NPF2 also divides Scotland into five geographic areas:

- Central Belt
- East Coast
- Highlands and Islands
- Ayrshire and the South West
- South of Scotland

and identifies priorities and opportunities for each area.

The present phase of NPF2 is that of monitoring and evaluation. The action programme identifies the processes needed to deliver the strategy; how these contribute to the realisation of the strategy; key milestones in taking them forward; the bodies responsible for delivery and lead partners. The Monitoring Report for NPF2 will report on progress in delivering national developments. The present Scottish Government has committed to reviewing the NPF every 4 years.

Comment on NPF2

The publication of the second NPF in 2009 and the enhanced statutory status provided by the 2006 Act reforms have generally been welcomed. It accords with the European Spatial Development Perspective, which promotes the spatial planning approach to Member States. Within the UK, the three devolved administrations have developed national spatial frameworks. This has not been undertaken in England, where, under the Labour administration, a regional approach had been adopted. Some concerns, however, have been expressed about the process and the outcome of NPF2. There are two main strands to these criticisms: the first issue relates to involvement of the general public, the second to the lack of an independent scrutiny for the NPF. Each is briefly considered.

Public participation is shaped by the use of the participation statement, as there is no formal process of notification and advertisement. This is undoubtedly a weak legislative requirement, but it was defended by the then Scottish Minister for Communities, in the Stage 3 debate on the Bill. It was explained that while the NPF would be developed painstakingly over a prolonged period, with the full participation of the public, interested organisations and parliamentarians, "ultimately the national policy framework is a statement of Government policy, which is the responsibility of Scottish Ministers" (Official Report, 15 November 2006, col 29196). The participation statement may well turn out to be inclusive, transparent and robust, but, as Rowan Robinson observes, its requirements are framed in a way which would encompass both the best and the worst in participation practice (*The Town and Country Planning (Scotland) Act 1997* (Green's Annotated Acts, 2009), p x). Such a light touch regulatory regime for public involvement can enable flexibility and creativity in the engagement process. It was acknowledged, however, that there was room for improvement in the style and mechanisms for community involvement in the preparation of the future NPFs (Final NPF2 Participation Statement and Conformity Report, 2009).

Second, although under other legislation a Strategic Environmental Assessment and an Appropriate Assessment have been undertaken, there is no opportunity for an independent and professional scrutiny of the NPF. This is particularly important in relation to national developments. The significance of the designation, as the then Scottish Minister for Communities pointed out during the Stage 3 debate, is that, "designation as a national development will establish the policy need for the development in question" (col 29187). In other words, as Rowan Robinson explains:

> "the need for the development will not be a matter for debate during any subsequent site authorisation process. While it is appropriate that the final word on designation of national developments should rest with Scottish Ministers, it will be important that communities, who may eventually be faced with the location of such a development in their area, should have confidence in the process, leading to designation, including the process for assessing need for the development" (*The Town and Country Planning (Scotland) Act 1997* (Green's Annotated Acts, 2009), p x).

In the creation of NPF2, the national developments were altered and augmented after the 60-day period of laying the proposed NPF before the Scottish Parliament.

At the time of writing, a petition seeking judicial review of the designation by Scottish Ministers of a new power station and transhipment hub at Hunterston, as a national development in the National Planning Framework, has been lodged by way of a judicial review application in the Court of Session and awaits determination. The outcome of this case may have implications for the process of preparing the NPF, in particular the level of public participation and the issue as to whether there should be some form of independent scrutiny of the proposals.

SCOTTISH PLANNING POLICY

The UK planning system is characterised by the provision of generic policy on planning and Scotland has been at the forefront of this, prompted originally by the need to deal with the unprecedented problems posed by the siting of onshore developments associated with oil and gas exploration (Scottish Office, North Sea Oil and Gas Coastal Planning Guidelines (1974)). National planning guidelines on other topics followed, as the benefits of the system became apparent. Over the years, central policy advice has taken several formats and been given various titles, most recently Scottish Planning Policies (SPPs). These have now been consolidated into *Scottish Planning Policy* (2010), a single statement of the Scottish Government's strategy for Scotland's long-term spatial development (Scottish Government, *Scottish Planning Policy* (February 2010)). It contains the following:

- the Scottish Government's view of the purpose of planning;
- the core principles for the operation of the system and the objectives for key parts of the system;
- statutory guidance on sustainable development and planning; and
- concise subject planning policies, including the implications for development planning and development management.

There is no reference to Scottish Planning Policy in the legislation; however, the policies expressed in the SPP should inform the content of development plans: local development plans and strategic development plans. Relevant parts of this policy document must be considered as part of the decision-making process on a planning application, as the SPP is a material consideration in the determination of planning applications and "should be used to inform development proposals from initial concept to implementation" (*Scottish Planning Policy* (2010), para 2).

The SPP also contains guidance on sustainable development. The 2006 Act reforms introduced a requirement that functions relating to the preparation of the NPF by Scottish Ministers and development plans by planning authorities must be exercised with the objective of contributing to sustainable development. Planning authorities are to have regard to guidance on this requirement issued by Scottish Ministers (1997 Act, s 3E), which is provided by paras 34–40 of *Scottish Planning Policy* (2010). There is also a section that deals with climate change and planning, including the responsibilities for public bodies under the Climate Change (Scotland) Act 2009.

Scottish Planning Policy: subject policies

The subject policies in the SPP are as follows:

- Economic Development;
- Town Centres and Retailing;
- Housing;
- Rural Development;
- Coastal Planning;
- Fish Farming;
- Historic Environment;
- Landscape and Natural Heritage;

- Open Space and Physical Activity;
- Green Belts;
- Transport;
- Renewable Energy;
- Flooding and Drainage;
- Waste Management;
- Minerals;
- Onshore Oil and Gas operations;
- Surface Coal Mining;
- Communications Infrastructure.

The SPP is available at: http://www.scotland.gov.uk/Publications/2010/02/03132605/0.

Designing Places: a policy statement for Scotland (2001)

This statement sets out aspirations on design and the role of the planning system in delivering this. Its aim is to contribute to raising standards of design in both urban and rural areas. The 2006 Act reforms introduced a requirement to submit design statements, as part of the planning application process for some applications. *Designing Places* provides guidance on the preparation and content of these statements. It is available at: http://www.scotland.gov.uk/library3/planning/dpps-00.asp.

Designing Streets (2010)

This is a policy statement for street design. It advocates a design-led approach aimed at improving the quality of design in urban and rural development. It is available at: http://www.scotland.gov.uk/Publications/2010/03/22120652/3.

Circulars

Scottish Government circulars form a miscellaneous category of quasi-legislation, comprising a variety of advice and guidance. Planning circulars have been issued on many topics over the years and play an important role in the day-to-day operation of the planning system (eg Circular 1/2009: *Development Planning* and Circular 8/2007: *The Environmental Impact Assessment (Scotland) Regulations 1999*). Circulars cannot vary statute or case law, but contain guidance on policy implementation through legislative or procedural change. There are some examples of variance between judicial decisions and the circular advice (eg Circular 4/1998: *The Use of Conditions in Planning Permissions* and Circular 1/2010:

Planning Agreements). Circulars cannot be enforced; however, non-compliance with a planning circular contributing to a refusal of planning permission may result in the reversal of the decision at appeal. A full list of current circulars is available at: http://www.scotland.gov.uk/Topics/Built-Environment/planning/publications/circulars/Q/editmode/on/forceupdate/on.

Planning Advice Notes

Planning Advice Notes (PANs) are another notable feature of the Scottish planning system and cover a wide variety of topics. PANs provide advice and information on technical planning matters (eg PAN 50: *Controlling the Environmental Effects of Surface Mineral Workings* and PAN 70: *Electronic Planning Service Delivery*). They also include good practice advice in the form of photographs or visual representations (eg PAN 72: *Housing in the Countryside*). The advice is indicative and aimed at improving practice; it does not have to be followed by either planning authorities or developers. The topics covered and the nature of the advice, however, mean that in practice the advice is often adopted by those using the planning system. A full list of PANs is available at: http://www.scotland.gov.uk/Topics/Built-Environment/planning/publications/pans/Q/editmode/on/forceupdate/on.

An undertaking to scale back the amount of planning advice issued by Scottish Ministers (*Modernising the Planning System* (2008)) will eventually result in an overall reduction in the number of PANs. There will also be an increased focus on technical matters. The proposed approach to the Planning Advice Notes is available at: http://www.scotland.gov.uk/Topics/Built-Environment/planning/publications/pans/Approach. This includes a list of PANs to be retained in their current form; those to be updated and merged in 2010; those to be updated in 2011; and those to be revoked.

COMMENT ON NATIONAL PLANNING POLICY

The last few years have seen a rationalisation and streamlining of policy formulation at national level. This has accompanied the reform of the planning system and has contributed to the overall aim of the 2005 White Paper to implement culture change in the planning process, through non-legislative measures (p 31). It has also been a function of the devolved administration, that planning policy has been developed in a particularly Scottish way. The development of the National Planning Framework is the most obvious example of this. It does, however, appear to mark a shift of power from local authorities to the Scottish Government. It will be interesting to follow the consent processes for national developments over the next few years. It is particularly important that the NPF does not become a means of fast tracking controversial proposals.

Essential Facts

National Planning Framework

- The National Planning Framework (NPF) is the Scottish Government's strategy for long-term spatial development to 2030.
- It is required by s 3A(1) of the 1997 Act: "there is to be a spatial plan for Scotland".
- The NPF can identify National Developments under s 3A(4)(b) of the 1997 Act.
- In identifying a National Development, the NPF must state the need for that development.
- The NPF must be taken into account in preparing development plans.
- The NPF is a material consideration in determining planning applications.
- The principle of a national development will not be overturned by a subsequent consent process for the development.
- Scotland has had policy guidance on planning since the 1970s, although it is not a statutory requirement.

Scottish Government Planning Guidance

- *Scottish Planning Policy* (SPP) (2010) has updated and consolidated the guidance into one document. It covers the operation of the planning system; provides statutory guidance on sustainable development and planning and gives subject-specific advice (eg renewable energy).
- Scottish Government Guidance is also contained in *Designing Places* (2001) and *Designing Streets* (2010).
- Planning Circulars provide advice and guidance and many have been issued to accompany the implementation of the 2006 Act reforms.
- Planning Advice Notes (PANs) provide good practice advice on technical planning matters. The Scottish Government is in the process of updating the PANs series.

4 LOCAL PLANNING POLICY

The previous chapter noted that the planning process is characterised by the central role of policy and guidance. The development plan has been the main way of providing this at local level since the Town and Country Planning (Scotland) Act 1947 imposed a duty on every planning authority to prepare a development plan. This is consistent with local authorities having the primary responsibility for the operation of the planning system (*Scottish Planning Policy* (2010), para 8). This chapter explains the background to reform of the development plan system. It explains the requirements of the new regime and the associated process of Strategic Environmental Assessment (SEA). It concludes with some reflection on the reform to the development plan system in Scotland.

The nature of the development plan has changed over the years and the system has been altered again by the 2006 Act reforms. The existing two-tier regime of structure and local plans is replaced with two new forms of plan: strategic development plans (SDPs) and local development plans (LDPs). The development plan, in future, will comprise of a local development plan supported by supplementary guidance. In the four largest city regions, the development plan is also compromised of a strategic development plan, which addresses land use issues that cross local authority boundaries or involve strategic infrastructure (*Scottish Planning Policy* (2010), para 10). The new system of development planning became operational in February 2009; however, the changes will take time to take effect, as they involve alterations to the way in which the plans are prepared. Although planning authorities have commenced their preparation, fully operational new style plans are some years away. There will effectively, therefore, be two separate systems running in tandem (Planning etc (Scotland) Act 2006 (Development Planning) (Saving, Transitional and Consequential Provisions) Order 2008 (SSI 2009/18)). This text deals only with the new arrangements (see, eg, J Rowan Robinson *et al*, *Scottish Planning Law and Procedure* (2001) for a comprehensive description of the old structure and local plan regime).

BACKGROUND TO REFORM

Planning authorities are required to have regard to the development plan in the determination of planning applications. A plan-led system was first introduced in 1994; thereafter, "where, in making any determination under the planning Acts, regard is to be had to the development plan, the determination is, unless material considerations indicate otherwise – (a) to be made in accordance with the plan" (1997 Act, s 25(1)(a)). One of the aims of the White Paper, *Modernising the Planning System* (2005) was to make the plan-led system more robust. Development plans are often out of date and the White Paper noted that 70 per cent of local plans had been adopted more than 5 years earlier and that 20 per cent had been adopted more than 15 years earlier (p 12). This problem has been compounded by delays in the preparation of new development plans. The primacy of the development plan in the system has therefore been weakened, leading to increasing uncertainty and lack of confidence on the part of both communities and businesses (M Poustie, "Planning Reforms in Scotland" (2007) *JPL* 489 at 494). It was recognised in 2000 that continuation of the *status quo* was not an option and that the "wicked issues" on strategic planning had to be tackled (speech by Sam Galbraith MSP, Minister for the Environment, RTPI Annual Conference, Aberdeen (2000)). A consultation process followed: *Review of Strategic Planning* (2001) and *Making Development Plans Deliver* (2004); and it revealed clear support for improving the development planning regime. The proposals for change were ultimately set out in the White Paper, *Modernising the Planning System* (2005). These included proposals: "to place development plans at the heart of the system"; "to encourage greater efficiency in development plan preparation"; and "to make it easier for people to get involved in planning and help shape the future of their communities" (*Modernising the Planning System*, p 8). The specific proposals included a new regime of development plans, combined with procedures aimed at streamlining the preparation process, as well as requiring regular review.

SUSTAINABLE DEVELOPMENT

The 2006 Act reforms introduce a duty that functions relating to the preparation of development plans by planning authorities, like those relating to the preparation of the NPF by Scottish Ministers, must be exercised with the objective of contributing to sustainable development (1997 Act, s 3E(2)). The 2006 Act reforms also require that regard must be had to any guidance issued by Scottish Ministers (1997 Act, s 3D(3)) and such guidance on the sustainable development requirement is contained within *Scottish Planning Policy* (2010) (paras 34–40).

The question of the incorporation of sustainable development, as a purpose for planning, was debated during the passage of the Planning and

Compulsory Purchase Bill through the Westminster Parliament; however, the subsequent Act (the Planning and Compulsory Purchase Act 2004) merely provided that the person or body (exercising a development plan function) must exercise that function with the objective of contributing to sustainable development (2004 Act, s 39(4)). Furthermore, the Government resisted pressure to add a definition of sustainable development; authorities were instead to be referred to guidance to be issued by the Secretary of State. The combination of environmental, social and economic matters means that almost any project, falling short of wanton vandalism, is capable of being described as sustainable (Tromans *et al*, *Planning and Compulsory Purchase Act 2004, A Guide to the New Law* (2005), p 63). Ross concludes that the 2004 Act requirements established sustainable development as a primary duty for the relevant public body, which has priority over other duties and objectives ("Why legislate for sustainable development? An examination of sustainable development provisions in UK and Scottish statutes" *J Env L* 35 at 53). She points out, however, that this duty is confined to development planning functions and notes this was the subject of debate during the Bill's passage.

In Scotland, striking the appropriate balance between the different elements of sustainable development is now squarely in the hands of the Government (J Rowan Robinson, *The Town and Country Planning (Scotland) Act 1997* (Green's Annotated Acts, 2009, p xi)). The restriction of the requirement to contribute to sustainable development to NPF and development plan functions was also part of the debate in the Scottish Parliament, including whether it should have been extended to development management functions. This was considered on a number of occasions, but was ultimately rejected. The Policy Memorandum explains that the application of the requirement would be problematic because it would be too difficult to determine, with legal certainty, whether or not the developments proposed were sustainable (para 27). However, Rowan Robinson observes that, given the primacy of development plans, there should be a trickle down effect into development management (p xiii).

DEVELOPMENT PLAN PREPARATION

Development Plan Schemes

The starting point for plan preparation under the new regime is a Development Plan Scheme. Each planning authority and Strategic Development Plan Authority (SDPA) is to prepare, at least once a year, a Development Plan Scheme (1997 Act, s 20B). This sets out the authority's programme for preparing and reviewing its plans and what is likely to be involved at each stage. It must include a participation statement, stating when, how and with whom consultation on the plan will take place, and the authority's proposals for public involvement in the plan process (Planning Circular 1/2009: *Development Planning*, para 7). Scottish Ministers expect "participation statements to contain a range of innovative techniques and activities for consulting stakeholders tailored to local circumstances and the issues being dealt with in the plan" (Circular 1/2009, para 7). The Development Plan Scheme must also contain a timetable, specifying the month the authority proposes to publish its next main issues report, proposed plan and to submit the proposed plan to Scottish Ministers (Town and Country Planning (Development Planning) (Scotland) Regulations 2008, reg 24). There is no requirement to consult on the Development Plan Scheme, but, once the scheme has been adopted, there are statutory publicity requirements. All authorities in Scotland had published Development Plan Schemes by March 2009.

STRATEGIC DEVELOPMENT PLANS (SDPs)

This section sets out the requirements for preparation of an SDP. This is also illustrated by the diagram below. Scottish Ministers expect SDPs to be concise, visionary documents that set clear parameters for subsequent LDPs and inform decisions about strategic infrastructure investment.

Strategic Development Plan Authority

The SDPA has the responsibility for preparing the Strategic Development Plan (1997 Act, s 4(1)). The SDPA Designation Orders established SDPAs in Glasgow, Aberdeen, Dundee and Edinburgh city regions. These came into existence and have been operating with dedicated staff since 2008. Their first task was to submit a proposal for a strategic development plan area.

Strategic Development Plan Area

A plan showing the proposed boundary of the Strategic Development Plan Area and a statement in justification of it, was submitted to Scottish Ministers within 3 months of the designation of the SDPAs. Scottish Ministers could then determine that the boundary of the strategic development plan area was to be:

Strategic Development Plan process

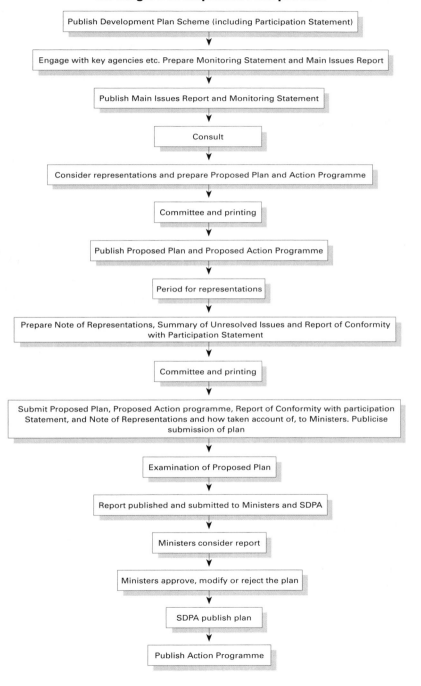

- the boundary proposed in the submission;
- the proposed boundary with such modifications as they thought fit; or
- such other boundary as they thought fit (1997 Act, ss 5–6).

A determination by Scottish Ministers on the boundary of the Strategic Development Plan Authority Area is final.

SDP: form and content

The SDP consists of two main elements: a vision statement and a spatial strategy. It must also contain a map or diagram (or a combination of the two) illustrating the spatial strategy.

Vision statement

A vision statement is a broad statement of the SDPA's views as to how the development of the Strategic Development Plan Area could and should occur, including matters which might be expected to affect development (1997 Act, s 7(4) and Planning Circular 1/2009, para 13). Vision statements should provide a realistic expression of what the plan area could be like in 20 years' time and a useful springboard for the spatial strategy of the plan.

The principal topics for SDPs are listed in Planning Circular 1/2009, para 15, as follows:

- land for housing;
- land for business;
- land for shopping development;
- waste management development;
- strategic infrastructure (including transport, water supply and waste water);
- strategic greenspace networks (including greenbelts).

SDP: preparation

There are 15 stages from initial survey of the SDP area to creation of the first SDP through to review associated with the second and subsequent SDPs.

The stages are as follows:

(1) monitoring and the evidence base for the SDP;
(2) publication of the main issues report and monitoring statement;
(3) consultation/period for representations (6 weeks);

(4) preparation of proposed plan and action programme;

(5) publication of proposed plan and action programme;

(6) consultation period (6–12 weeks);

(7) preparation of note of representations, summary of unresolved issues and report on conformity with participation statement. Modification of the proposed plan;

(8) submission of the proposed plan, proposed action programme, report on conformity with participation statement and note of how representations had been taken into account to Ministers, and publicising submission of plan;

(9) examination;

(10) report on examination to Scottish Ministers;

(11) decision on SDP;

(12) SDPA publishes plan;

(13) action programme;

(14) monitoring;

(15) review every 4 years.

Monitoring and the evidence base for SDP

The first stage in the SPD preparation is the collection of basic data and consultation with key agencies and others in line with the participation statement outlined in the development plan scheme. The survey process does not have to be undertaken entirely from scratch, as all SDP areas have previously been covered by structure plans and monitoring of the physical environment for strategic planning proposals has been ongoing since 1976. Nevertheless, monitoring changes in the principal physical, economic, social and environmental characteristics of the SDP area; and the impact of the policies and proposals of the existing plan(s) are required to produce a monitoring statement (1997 Act, s 4(10)). This is to be published at the same time as the main issues report.

The purpose of the main issues report is to facilitate and inform the preparation of the SDP. It sets out the authority's general proposals for development in the area (1997 Act, s 9(1) and (2)) and proposals as to where development should and should not occur (1997 Act, s 9(2)(a)). It should be sufficiently clear and precise to enable people to understand what is being proposed and to make meaningful comments (Circular 1/2009, para 17). It will also contain one or more reasonable alternative sets of proposals (1997 Act, s 9(2)(b)) and it should draw attention to the ways in which the favoured and alternative proposals differ from the spatial strategy of the existing approved SDP (if any) (1997 Act, s 9(3)(b)).

In preparing the main issues report, the SDPA must take account of the NPF (1997 Act, s 8(1)(a)). SDPAs are also required to consult with and have regard to the views of:

• the key agencies,
• the neighbouring planning authorities,
• Scottish Ministers,
• such persons as may be prescribed.

It is the duty of a key agency to co-operate with the SDPA in the compilation of the main issues report (1997 Act, s 9(5)).

The SDPA must also consider, according to para 16 of Planning Circular 1/2009:

• the resources available for carrying out the policies and proposals in the plan;
• any approved or proposed SDP for a neighbouring SDP area;
• any regional transport strategy, river basin management plan or local housing strategy relating to the area;
• the national waste management plan; and
• issues arising out of the European directive on the control of major accident hazards involving dangerous substances.

Scottish Ministers may require that preparation of the SDP is to be completed by a specified date (1997 Act, s 8(2)).

Publication of the main issues report

The monitoring and evaluation exercises together with the consultation and participation process results in the creation of the main issues report and the monitoring statement. Publication of the main issues report is the second important stage in the SDP process. It is also a key stage for the Strategic Environmental Assessment (SEA) (see below for more detail on SEA). The minimum publication requirements are set out in Circular 1/2009 (reg 5). Information is published in a local newspaper circulating in the SDP Area and on the internet as follows:

• advising that the main issues report has been prepared and where and when it may be inspected;
• a brief description of its content and purpose;

- details of how further information may be obtained;
- a statement that any person wishing to do so may make representations on the content of the main issues report; and
- information as to how, when and to whom any representations should be made.

A notice containing this information must be sent to:

- the key agencies;
- an SDPA or a planning authority for land which adjoins the strategic development plan area; and
- any community council, any part of whose area is within the strategic development plan area.

A copy of the main issues report must be made available for inspection at each of the planning authorities comprising the strategic development planning authority and in every public library, as well as being published on the internet.

The SDPA must also ensure that people who may be expected to want to comment on the main issues report are made aware that they can do so and are given such an opportunity (Circular 1/2009, para 20). A copy of the published main issues report and the monitoring statement must also be sent to Scottish Ministers (1997 Act, s 9(9)).

Consultation on the main issues report
A 6-week consultation period follows the publication of the main issues report (Circular 1/2009, para 23).

Proposed Strategic Development Plan
A proposed SDP is then prepared, having regard to the representations submitted on the main issues report (1997 Act, s 10). An action programme for implementation of the SDP is also prepared at the same time. The proposed SDP will require SDPA committee approval.

Publication of the proposed SDP and proposed action programme
A proposed SDP is then published.

Consultation
The proposed SDP is subject to the same publicity requirements as the main issues report and there must be at least a 6-week period for submission

of representations (Circular 1/2009, para 19). Circular 1/2009 suggests that SDPAs may consider offering a longer period of up to 12 weeks for complex plans, to give parties sufficient time to formulate the entirety of their case (para 55). Copies of the proposed SDP must be sent to the key agencies and neighbouring planning authorities. People who commented on the main issues report are to be notified of where and when they can inspect the proposed plan. The SDPA is also to consult the key agencies and Scottish Ministers.

Interestingly, Planning Circular 1/2009 states that Scottish Ministers expect the proposed plan to represent the planning authority's settled view on the final adopted content of the plan. This stage should not be to "test the water": as new or controversial elements of the plan content should already have been aired at the main issues report stage, at least as options or alternatives. The Circular also states that representations should be concise (ie no more than 2,000 words, plus any limited supporting productions), but should fully explain the issues that people wish to be considered at a subsequent examination. This is because there is no automatic opportunity for parties to expand on their representations later in the process (para 55).

Assessment of representations and consultation responses and preparation of modifications (if required)

The SDPA prepares a note of all the representations, indicating whether and to what extent representations were taken into account in the plan (1997 Act, s 10(3)(b)(i)), together with a report comparing the participation statement with the actual participation process undertaken by the SDPA (1997 Act, s 10(3)(b)(ii)). Circular 1/2009 states that it would also be sensible for the SDPA to submit a summary of unresolved issues (para 26).

It is clear that Scottish Ministers expect the authority's progress to be as quick as possible. Circular 1/2009 points out that pre-examination negotiations and notifiable modifications can cause significant delay and, therefore, are not to be undertaken as a matter of course, but only where the authority is minded to make significant changes to the plan. Nevertheless, representations and consultation responses received on the proposed plan may result in the modification of the proposed SDP. If the modifications are so significant as to change the underlying aims or strategy of the plan, the SDPA must prepare and publish a new proposed plan, with all the associated consultation requirements (1997 Act, s 10(3)(b)(i)).

SDP: submission to Scottish Ministers

The next stage is submission of the proposed SDP to Scottish Ministers, which must be accompanied by a note of the representations. The publicity requirements include the publication of a notice in at least one local newspaper and on the internet, stating that the proposed plan has been submitted to Scottish Ministers, the date of submission and details of when and where the plan may be inspected (Town and Country Planning (Development Planning) (Scotland) Regulations 2008, reg 7). The notice must also be sent to the key agencies and people who submitted representations on the plan. A copy of the submitted plan must be available for inspection in planning offices, public libraries and on the internet.

In the event that the planning authorities that constitute the SDPA cannot agree on the plan's content, s 11 of the 1997 Act allows the submitted plan to contain alternative proposals, together with the reasoning behind them.

Examination

The 2006 Act reforms provide for compulsory examination of both strategic development plans and local development plans (1997 Act, ss 12, 12A, 19 and 19A). Examinations are intended as the principal means of independently testing the issues arising from representations on proposed strategic development plans and local development plans.

According to Circular 1/2009, para 68, the examination is expected to be:

- succinct and proportionate;
- focused on the examiner seeking out the information;
- an examination of the issues raised, rather than a response to each individual representation;
- a process that is understandable and transparent to the public.

The intention is that, where appropriate, more user-friendly methods than the public inquiry are to be employed (Rowan Robinson, *The Town and Country Planning (Scotland) Act 1997*, p xiii).

On receiving the proposed SDP, Scottish Ministers are required (by virtue of the 1997 Act, s 12(1)) to appoint an examiner for the plan where:

- there are unresolved representations;
- the proposed plan contains alternative proposals; or
- Scottish Ministers otherwise consider an examination to be appropriate.

A key principle of the revised examination procedure is that, as far as possible, the examiner should be supplied with all the information from the outset.

Provision of information to the examiner   The SDPA is required to supply the following material to the examiner within 14 days of being notified of their appointment:

- a summary of unresolved issues;
- copies of the unresolved representations;
- the environmental report;
- the proposed action programme;
- the monitoring statement; and
- the participation statement current when the proposed plan was published.

There is no provision for those who have made representations or the SDPA to submit further material to the examination beyond this process, unless required to do so by the appointed person. This is an important shift of emphasis and reinforces the front loading of the process (Circular 1/2009, para 72).

Examination of conformity with the participation statement   The first act of the examiner is to consider the implementation of the participation statement and take a view on whether the authority has consulted on the plan and involved the public, according to it (Circular 1/2009, paras 85–88). If it is concluded that there were shortcomings in compliance, this is reported to Scottish Ministers with recommendations on the further steps the authority should take with regard to consultation or public involvement. However, it is expected that these procedures will rarely, if ever, be brought into play.

Scope of examination   Examinations are limited by s 12(1) of the 1997 Act and reg 21 of the Town and Country Planning (Development Planning) (Scotland) Regulations 2008 to three main areas:

- issues raised in representations;
- alternative proposals arising from the planning authorities that constitute the SDPA being unable to agree on content;
- any matters highlighted by the Scottish Ministers in appointing an examiner.

Regulation 21 deliberately intends to prevent the scope of the examination spreading to become a wider test of the soundness of the plan. The reporter is not tasked with making the plan as good as it can be, but with modifying those parts that are clearly inappropriate or insufficient (Circular 1/2009, para 78).

Examination procedure In line with the move to adopt more user-friendly methods of examination, it is the examiner who will determine the form of the examination and, in particular, whether the examination is to be held in public, and whether participants are to rely on written submissions or be given an opportunity to be heard. The options for examination can include inquiry sessions, hearings and written submissions, or be comprised of a range of these or other methods. It is expected that different aspects of individual issues may be dealt with using a number of formats, and decisions on the format will be at the discretion of the examiner. For example, where an oral session is requested it is anticipated that this will normally follow the hearing format, rather than a formal inquiry session (Circular 1/2009, para 81). The examiner can request further representations or information from any person, in order to make a proper assessment of an issue (Town and Country Planning (Development Planning) (Scotland) Regulations 2008, reg 22). It is expected that where further evidence is requested, this will normally be in written form.

Post-examination procedures A report is prepared upon conclusion of the examination, which will include conclusions and recommendations for each of the issues identified at the start of the examination process, but not on each individual representation. The report will also set out the examiner's assessment of the authority's conformity with the participation statement. The report is published, submitted to Scottish Ministers and sent to the SDPA. Those who made unresolved representations are also notified that the report has been published and submitted to Scottish Ministers (Circular 1/2009, paras 82–83).

SDP: decision

Scottish Ministers make the final decision on the SDP. This decision is made upon conclusion of the examination and the submission of the report to Scottish Ministers. If there is no examination, the decision is made upon receipt of the proposed SDP from the SDPA. Scottish Ministers can approve or reject the plan (1997 Act, s 13). Where the plan is approved, this may be either in whole or in part. Scottish Ministers may also approve a modified plan. There are various procedures for making modifications (1997 Act, s 13(4)). Where there has been an examination, Scottish Ministers may make modifications in approving the plan, and will set out the reasons for these (1997 Act, s 13(4)(a)). Where there has not been an examination, any modifications will be published, along with reasons for making them, and consultation will be undertaken as considered appropriate, but including with the key agencies and the SDPA. In these circumstances there will be an opportunity to make representations on the modifications, prior to Ministers approving the plan. Scottish Ministers will notify the SDPA of any such representations, and may make further modifications in the light of these representations (1997 Act, s 13(4)–(8)). Once approved, the proposed plan is constituted as the Strategic Development Plan (1997 Act, s 13(2)).

Publication of the approved plan

Once the SDP has been approved, the SDPA is required, as soon as reasonably practicable, to publish it, including electronically, and two copies should be sent to Scottish Ministers (1997 Act, s 14).

Implementation of the SDP

The SDP will be implemented by the policies and proposals in the LDP, which is discussed next. It should be reviewed every 5 years. The role of monitoring, and the action plan, which also apply to the LDP, are discussed below.

LOCAL DEVELOPMENT PLAN

This section sets out the requirements for preparation of a Local Development Plan (LDP). This is also illustrated by the diagram below. LDPs must cover the whole of the planning authority's area and all planning authorities are required to prepare one or more LDPs, as soon as is practicable after implementation of the relevant part of the 2006 Act (28 February 2009). Initially, this will result in a degree of twin tracking in the SDP and LDP preparation; however, Scottish Ministers expect LDPs in SDP areas to be adopted within 2 years of the approval of the relevant SDP. The LDP main issues reports or proposed plans may be published on the basis of a proposed SDP, but the LDP should not be submitted to Scottish Ministers until the SDP has been approved (Circular 1/2009, para 33).

Local Development Plan process

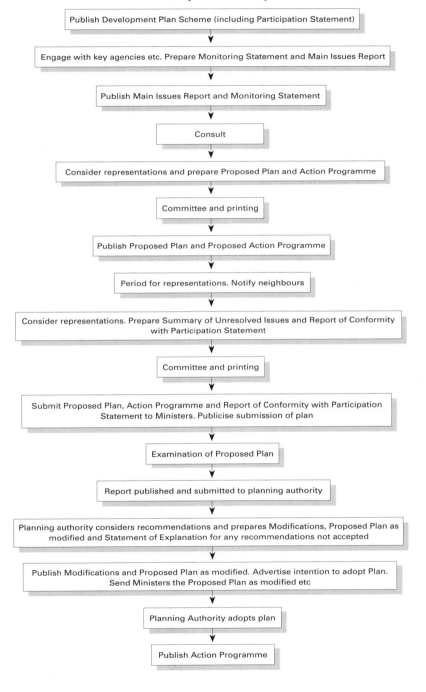

Publish Development Plan Scheme (including Participation Statement)

↓

Engage with key agencies etc. Prepare Monitoring Statement and Main Issues Report

↓

Publish Main Issues Report and Monitoring Statement

↓

Consult

↓

Consider representations and prepare Proposed Plan and Action Programme

↓

Committee and printing

↓

Publish Proposed Plan and Proposed Action Programme

↓

Period for representations. Notify neighbours

↓

Consider representations. Prepare Summary of Unresolved Issues and Report of Conformity with Participation Statement

↓

Committee and printing

↓

Submit Proposed Plan, Action Programme and Report of Conformity with Participation Statement to Ministers. Publicise submission of plan

↓

Examination of Proposed Plan

↓

Report published and submitted to planning authority

↓

Planning authority considers recommendations and prepares Modifications, Proposed Plan as modified and Statement of Explanation for any recommendations not accepted

↓

Publish Modifications and Proposed Plan as modified. Advertise intention to adopt Plan. Send Ministers the Proposed Plan as modified etc

↓

Planning Authority adopts plan

↓

Publish Action Programme

LPD: form and content

The LDP consists of two essential elements:

- a written part containing policies and proposals; and
- a map illustrating the proposals.

LDPs are to be concise map-based documents that focus on specific proposals over a 10-year time span (Circular 1/2009, para 39). Outside SDP areas, they are expected to provide a broad indication of the scale and location of growth over a 20-year period. The Circular also anticipates that minor proposals and detailed policies may be removed to supplementary guidance, especially if there is no significant change from the previous plan, and provided an appropriate context remains in the plan itself. Supplementary guidance is also to be used to complement and update the new development plans. (See below for more detail on supplementary guidance.) In SDP areas, LDPs need not repeat policy material contained in the SDP.

LDP: preparation

There are 16 possible stages from initial survey of the LDP area through to adoption of the plan and on to monitoring and review associated with the second and subsequent LDPs.

The stages are as follows:

(1) monitoring and the evidence base for the LDP;
(2) publication of the main issues report and monitoring statement;
(3) consultation and period for representations (6 weeks);
(4) preparation of proposed plan and action programme;
(5) publication of proposed plan and proposed action programme;
(6) consultation and notification period (6–12 weeks);
(7) preparation of note of representations, summary of unresolved issues and report on conformity with participation statement;
(8) submission of the proposed plan, proposed action programme, report on conformity with participation statement and note of how representations had been taken into account to Ministers, and publicising submission of plan;
(9) examination;
(10) report published and submitted to planning authority;
(11) planning authority considers recommendations and prepares modifications, proposed plan as modified and statement of explanation for any recommendations not accepted;

(12) publication of modifications and proposed plan as modified and statement of explanation for any recommendations not accepted;

(13) planning authority adopts plan;

(14) action programme;

(15) monitoring;

(16) review: every 5 years.

Monitoring and the evidence base for the LDP

Planning authorities are required to compile a main issues report as part of the process for preparing the LDP. It is also a key stage for the Strategic Environmental Assessment (SEA) (see below for more detail on SEA). The main issues report uses information based on monitoring of the LDP area and building on the planning data collated for previous local plans, over many years. LDPs should be fully co-ordinated with other key strategies from the earliest stage, "with key infrastructure providers signed up to the delivery of the emerging proposals" (Circular 1/2009, para 44). The planning authority must, therefore, consult with and have regard to any views expressed by Scottish Ministers, the key agencies, any adjoining planning authority (including national park authorities) and any planning authority within the same SDPA as the LDP area (1997 Act, s 17(4) and the Town and Country Planning (Development Planning) (Scotland) Regulations 2008, reg 11). It is considered that the main issues report should be an engaging document that encourages the public and other stakeholders to read and respond to it. In particular, publication should come before the planning authority has reached a firm view as to the strategy to be followed and the authority's approach should not be one of defending its proposals, but one of genuine openness to ideas (Circular 1/2009, para 46).

Publication of the main issues report and monitoring statement

The main issues report is then published with a monitoring statement.

Consultation on the main issues report

A 6-week consultation period follows the publication of the LDP main issues report. The publication requirements for the main issues report are set out by reg 12 of the Town and Country Planning (Development Planning) (Scotland) Regulations 2008. This includes publication of notices in a local newspaper circulating in the area and on the internet; and sending a notice to the key agencies, adjoining planning authorities and relevant community councils. The main issues report must be available at an office of the planning authority and in every public library in the LDP area. It must also be published on the internet.

Preparation of proposed Local Development Plan

The planning authority must have regard to the representations received on the main issues report in preparing the proposed LDP and associated action programme. Scottish Ministers expect the proposed plan to represent the planning authority's settled view as to what the final adopted content of the plan should be (Circular 1/2009, para 55).

Publication of the proposed plan and action programme

Publication of the proposed LDP is subject to the same minimum publicity requirements as the main issues report (Town and Country Planning (Development Planning) (Scotland) Regulations 2008). In addition, the planning authority must consult with Scottish Ministers and key agencies.

Notification of sites in the LDP

An important new procedural requirement is that owners/occupiers of sites identified in the proposed LDP, which, if implemented, would be likely to have a significant effect on the use or amenity of that site or of neighbouring land are to be notified (Town and Country Planning (Development Planning) (Scotland) Regulations 2008, reg 14(1)). The notice is to be accompanied by a map showing the location of the site. The authority must allow at least 6 weeks for representations on the proposed plan, but this may be extended to 12 weeks.

Consideration by planning authority of consultation and notification responses

The next stage for the planning authority, following close of the consultation period on the proposed LDP, is to consider the representations, prepare a summary of unresolved issues and prepare a report on the conformity with the participation statement. Modifications may be made to the plan at this stage, but only to take account of representations, consultation responses or minor drafting or technical matters. It is considered that notifiable modifications (those that add, remove or significantly alter any policy or proposal in the plan) should not be undertaken as a matter of course, at this stage, but only where planning authorities are minded to make significant changes to the plan (Circular 1/2009, para 56).

There are four possible ways forward after the close of the period for representations:

(1) Where no representations have been received or all representations have been withdrawn or fully taken account of by non-notifiable modifications, the authority has to publish the plan and submit it to Scottish Ministers. The authority then has to advertise its intention to adopt it.

(2) Where there are unresolved representations, but the authority decides to make no notifiable modification, it has to publish the plan and submit it to Scottish Ministers.

(3) Where the authority decides to make notifiable modifications, it has to publish the modified plan and specify a date (at least 6 weeks ahead) by which further representations may be made. The authority may then further modify the plan or submit it to Scottish Ministers.

(4) Where the authority makes modifications that change the underlying aims or strategy of the proposed plan, it is required to prepare and publish a new proposed LDP.

Submission to Scottish Ministers

The LDP is then submitted to Scottish Ministers. The planning authority is also required to submit its proposed action programme, a report of conformity with its participation statement, and, if there are unresolved representations, a request that Scottish Ministers appoint a person to examine the proposed plan (1997 Act, ss 18(4) and 19(1)). There are also publicity requirements associated with this stage. Where no representations have been received, or all representations have been withdrawn or fully taken account of by non-notifiable modifications, and the authority publishes the plan at the same time as submission to Scottish Ministers, the planning authority has to advertise its intention to adopt the LDP.

Examination

Scottish Ministers will appoint a person to examine the LDP where there are unresolved representations. The examination process for LDPs is the same as for SDPs and is set out above.

Report published and submitted to planning authority

Upon conclusion of the examination, a report is submitted to the planning authority (Circular 1/2009, paras 82–83).

Response of planning authority to LDP examination report

Examination reports on LDPs are largely binding on planning authorities. The White Paper proposed this in order to promote greater confidence in the system and to reassure those who have participated in the plan-making process (p 29). Regulation 2 of the Town and Country Planning (Grounds for declining to follow recommendations) (Scotland) Regulations 2009 set out the circumstances when an authority can depart from recommendations in the examination report. Subject to these exceptions, s 19(10) of the 1997 Act requires authorities to make the modifications recommended and any other requisite modifications. The planning authority's power to depart from the recommendations of the examiner is, therefore, limited and this is another clear distinction from the previous regime.

Publication of modifications and proposed plan as modified

The planning authority then publishes the modifications and the plan, as it proposees to adopt it. It must also undertake the statutory publication and notification requirements (1997 Act, s 19(10) and the Town and Country Planning (Development Planning) (Scotland) Regulations 2008, reg 17).

Within 3 months of receiving the examination report, s 19(2) of the 1997 Act requires the authority to send to Scottish Ministers:

- the modifications made following receipt of the examination report;
- a statement setting out any recommended modifications that the authority has not made and the explanation for this;
- the proposed plan it wishes to adopt;
- the report of the examination;
- the advertisement of its intention to adopt the plan; and
- any environmental assessment carried out into the proposed plan as modified.

Adoption of the plan by the planning authority

The planning authority may adopt the plan after 28 days, unless directed not to by Scottish Ministers. Two copies of the adopted LDP must be sent to Scottish Ministers and various publicity and notification requirements must be undertaken (1997 Act, s 20A).

Action programmes

Planning authorities are required to prepare action programmes for both SDPs and LDPs. The proposed action programmes must be published and submitted to Scottish Ministers alongside proposed plans and must be adopted and published within 3 months of the plan being approved or adopted (1997 Act, s 21 and the Town and Country Planning (Development Planning) (Scotland) Regulations 2008, regs 25 and 26).

Monitoring

Monitoring is an ongoing process for both SDPs and LDPs which should focus on what has changed. It should set the direction for the future review of the plans.

The review

The LDP review should take place at least every 5 years.

REPLACEMENT OF PLANS (SDPs AND LDPs)

The faster preparation process for the new development plans is coupled with the reintroduction of a statutory duty for SDPs and LDPs to be replaced, within a prescribed period. This is every 4 years for SDPs (1997 Act, s 10(8)) and 5 years for LDPs, or whenever required to do so by Scottish Ministers (1997 Act, s 16(a)(i) and (ii)). However, no sanction is provided in the event of failure to comply with the timescale, but Scottish Ministers may require an explanation and may themselves exercise default powers. It has been noted by Rowan Robinson that, in the past, Scottish Ministers have never shown a willingness to exercise default powers, notwithstanding very significant delays in the development planning process (*The Town and Country Planning (Scotland) Act 1997*, p xii).

SUPPLEMENTARY GUIDANCE

The status of supplementary planning guidance has been enhanced by the 2006 Act reforms. The intention behind the change in the law is that much detailed material can be contained in supplementary guidance, allowing the plans themselves to focus on vision and the wider spatial strategy, as well as being kept up to date, and therefore, relevant and shorter. A programme of supplementary guidance is regarded by Scottish Ministers as a key element in the implementation of the development plans. Prior to the 2006 Act reforms, supplementary planning guidance had been increasingly utilised by planning authorities to provide relevant planning advice, particularly to update policies during the lifetime of a plan. Such guidance had the legal status of a "material consideration". However, the 2006 Act reforms enable supplementary guidance to form part of the development plan. *Scottish Planning Policy* (2010), para 20 states that such guidance should be derived from the plan and has also been the subject of discussion and engagement. It must be submitted to Scottish Ministers and a period of 28 days elapse before the supplementary guidance is adopted and issued (1997 Act, s 22(6)). At any time before the supplementary guidance is adopted, Scottish Ministers may require the planning authority to make such modifications or direct the authority not to adopt and issue it. It should not be applied to development proposals until it has been formally agreed by the authority, following consideration of comments and representations on the draft. Scottish Ministers will scrutinise the guidance before it can be adopted by the planning authority. It is anticipated, however, that this pre-adoption scrutiny will focus more on ensuring that the principles of good public involvement and a proper connection with the SDP or LDP have been achieved consistently, than on detailed policy content.

STRATEGIC ENVIRONMENTAL ASSESSMENT

Directive 2001/42/EC on Strategic Environmental Assessment requires that certain draft plans or programmes produced by government, at all levels, must be accompanied by an environmental report, setting out their likely effects on the environment. In relation to the planning system in Scotland, this includes the NPF, SDPs, LDPs and formal supplementary guidance (NPF2 was subjected to an SEA). The Environmental Assessment (Scotland) Act 2005, however, requires all plans, programmes and strategies prepared by Scottish public bodies and office holders to be subject to an environmental assessment. This goes beyond the requirements merely to implement the Directive, although financial and budgetary plans and those relating to national defence or civil emergency are excluded (2005 Act, s 4).

The new development planning regime in Scotland has been designed to accommodate the SEA process: "SEA must be built into the plan preparation process (and) has a positive role to play within this" (PAN 1/2010: *Strategic Environmental Assessment*, para 1.2). However, SEA is essentially a process or generic tool, which contributes to the integration of environmental considerations into preparation and adoption of plans and programmes with a view to promoting sustainable development (SEA Directive, art 1). Detailed information about screening and scoping, the role of the consultation authorities (CAs), public consultation and each stage of the development planning process has been provided in Planning Advice Note 1/2010. This refers to key milestones in the new development plan process and the links between the development of the SDP and the LDP and SEA. One important area is the main issues report as both of the new style plans must be accompanied by an environmental report at this stage. It is recognised that it may need to be revised and republished at later stages, to take account of any material changes in the plan (PAN 1/2010, para 4.10). The role of consultation on the environmental report, as well as the content of the emerging plans, is emphasised in the guidance. There are also clear post-adoption procedures and, in particular, monitoring of the significant environmental effects of the implementation of each plan and programme. The purpose is to identify unforeseen adverse effects at an early point in the process, with a view to taking appropriate remedial action (SEA Directive, art 10 and 2005 Act, s 19). Reid points out that the key test of SEA will be its effectiveness in monitoring the plans and policies and the willingness to undertake remedial action (C T Reid, *Nature Conservation* (3rd edn, 2009), para 8.3.18).

COMMENT ON REFORMS TO LOCAL PLANNING POLICY

The 2005 White Paper's aims to transform local planning policy in Scotland were ambitious. The 2006 Act reforms have provided a range of measures to facilitate plans being kept up to date, relevant, shorter and more targeted. There are also enhanced participation procedures and a strengthening of the plan-led system. This, however, will inevitably lead to tensions in the operation of the policy regime. Only implementation will reveal whether the competing objectives can operate together successfully. In particular, it will be interesting to observe if more meaningful engagement with both the public and developers can be achieved at the same time as streamlining the development plan process to enable investment and other decisions to be made.

Essential Facts

Development Plans
- All local planning authorities must prepare a development plan.
- The 2006 Act reforms change the development plan system in Scotland to:

- Local Development Plans (LDPs);
- Strategic Development Plans (SDPs);
- Supplementary Guidance.

- The NPF must be taken into account in preparing development plans.
- Functions relating to the development plan must be exercised with the objective of contributing to sustainable development.

Strategic Development Plans (SDPs)

- SDPs are strategic development plans and are in preparation by Strategic Development Plan Authorities in the city region areas of Edinburgh, Glasgow, Dundee and Aberdeen.
- SDPs provide a strategic vision for a geographical area for a 10- to 20-year period and must be replaced every 4 years.

Local Development Plans (LDPs)

- LDPs must be prepared for all parts of Scotland by local planning authorities. They will contain detailed plans and policies for a 5- to 10-year period and must be replaced every 5 years.
- LDPs must be consistent with SDPs where they cover the same area.
- Where there is no SDP the LDP must provide a vision statement for the area.

Supplementary Guidance

- Supplementary Guidance can now form part of the development plan. It must be subject to consultation and approved by Scottish Ministers.

Strategic Environmental Assessment

- SDPs and LDPs (and some Supplementary Guidance) will require Strategic Environmental Assessment (Directive 2001/42/EC and the Environmental Assessment (Scotland) Act 2005).

5 DEFINITION OF "DEVELOPMENT" AND THE NEED FOR PLANNING PERMISSION

Planning permission is required for "any development of land" (1997 Act, s 28(1)). This chapter considers the definition of development in the legislation and case law. It includes an overview of the provisions in secondary legislation which enable development to proceed without the requirement of express planning permission. It concludes with reference to the procedures for ascertaining whether planning permission is or should have been obtained.

DEVELOPMENT

Development is defined by s 26(1) of the 1997 Act as "the carrying out of building, engineering, mining or other operations in, on, over or under land, or the making of any material change in the use of any buildings or land, or the operation of a marine fish farm in the circumstances specified in section 26AA". The definition has two parts: operations and use (the fish farm element is self-contained and therefore not considered at this stage). It is possible for a proposal to fall into both criteria; however, only one of the two aspects needs to be present to be caught by the definition (*Parkes* v *Secretary of State for the Environment* (1978)). There has been much judicial interpretation on the meaning of development; however, it is still the case that "development" is a key word in the planners' vocabulary whose meaning has evolved and is still evolving. It is "impossible to ascribe to it any certain dictionary meaning and difficult to analyse it accurately from the statutory definition": *Coleshill & District Investment Co Ltd* v *Minister of Housing and Local Government* (1969), per Lord Wilberforce. Notwithstanding the statutory and judicial guidance, the question of whether a proposal amounts to "development" and therefore requires planning permission is one of particular facts and circumstances for the planning authority or for Scottish Ministers to determine, rather than a matter of law. It is not always easy to say whether a proposed action comes within the statutory definition of development (Rowan Robinson *et al*, *Scottish Planning Law and Procedure* (2001) at para 5.01).

OPERATIONS

"Operations" consist of activities which result in some physical alteration of land that has some degree of permanence in relation to the land itself

(*Parkes* v *Secretary of State for the Environment* (1978), per Lord Denning MR at 1311).

Building operations

Planning permission is required for building operations which include demolition, rebuilding, structural alterations of or additions to buildings and other operations normally undertaken by a builder (1997 Act, s 26(4)).

Engineering operations

Engineering operations are defined as operations usually undertaken by or under the supervision of an engineer or which would require engineering skills, irrespective as to whether an engineer is actually involved (*Fayrewood Fish Farms* v *Secretary of State for the Environment* (1984)) and include the laying out of means of access to roads (1997 Act, s 277).

Mining operations

Mining operations include, *inter alia*, the removal of material of any description from a mineral-working deposit (1997 Act, s 26(5)). Mining, however, is regarded as a continuous operation and special controls apply to this form of development outwith the scope of this text.

Other operations

There is no definition of what amounts to "other operations", but it does not refer to all other operations (*Cambridge City Council* v *Secretary of State for the Environment* (1992)). Other operations therefore include any form of operational development which does not fall within the other categories, but which a planning authority or Scottish Ministers might reasonably consider would require planning permission (N Collar, *Planning* (2nd edn, 1999), para 4.09).

MATERIAL CHANGE OF USE

"Use" refers to activities which are done in, alongside or on land, but which do not interfere with the actual physical characteristics of the land (*Parkes* v *Secretary of State for the Environment* (1978), per Lord Denning MR at 1311). In determining whether a change of use has taken place, establishing the planning unit is an essential starting point. In general, the larger the planning unit, the less likely that a change of use will be material (*Burdle* v *Secretary of State for the Environment* (1972)). Most commonly, the planning unit will be the unit of occupation. A delicatessen which has a few tables and chairs for customers can be regarded as part of a planning unit for a shop, rather than a separate use as a restaurant. If such an ancillary use is no longer subordinate and becomes a main use in its own right, then a material change of use has occurred (*Alexander Transport* v *Secretary of State for Scotland* (1974)). Intensification of a use can also amount to a material change of use (*Edsell Caravan Parks Ltd* v *Hemel Hempstead Rural District Council* (1966)).

EXCLUSIONS FROM THE DEFINITION OF DEVELOPMENT

Section 26(2) specifically excludes certain operations or uses of land from the definition of development. This includes maintenance and alterations which only affect the interior of the building or do not materially affect its exterior (1997 Act, s 26(2)(a)(i) and (ii)); road and sewer maintenance by a local authority and statutory undertaker (1997 Act, s 26(2)(b) and (c)). Uses within the curtilage of a dwelling house which are incidental to its use as a dwelling (1997 Act, s 26(2)(d)) are also excluded from the definition of development. Working from home will often be considered incidental to the use of a house as a dwelling: for example, a person using a laptop and a telephone within the house would not normally require to apply for planning permission for a change of use. This could be distinguished, however, from a domestic garage and driveway being utilised for car restoration and sales. Each case, however, will be considered on its own merits and it will be a matter of fact and degree, according to the circumstances. The demolition of any building specified in a direction by Scottish Ministers is also excluded from the definition of development (1997 Act, s 26(2)(g)).

Section 26 provides definitions and clarifies "for the avoidance of doubt" that both the use of a dwelling house as two or more separate dwelling houses and the deposit of refuse or waste material on land constitutes development (1997 Act, s 26(3)). Other definitions relate to building operations (1997 Act, s 26(4)) and mining operations (1997 Act, s 26(5)).

Agriculture and forestry

The most important exclusions from the definition of development are agriculture and forestry. The use of any land for the purposes of agriculture or forestry (including afforestation) and the use for any of those purposes of any building occupied together with land so used, are specifically excluded from the definition of development (1997 Act, s 26(2) (e)). This is important due to these uses being so significant in terms of Scotland's land mass. The definition of agriculture and, in particular, the application of this exclusion has resulted in a rich source of case law (see, eg, Rowan Robinson *et al*, *Scottish Planning Law and Procedure*, paras 5.142–5.148). Agriculture and forestry, however, are increasingly coming under planning authority control: for example, s 26(2)(a) extends the definition of development to include the carrying out of irrigation or drainage for agriculture. It should be noted that agriculture and forestry operations, within the meaning of "building, engineering, mining or other operations" (1997 Act, s 26(1)), constitute development requiring planning permission. Certain agricultural and forestry operational development, however, is granted a general planning permission by Classes 18 and 19 of the Schedule to the Town and Country Planning (General Permitted Development) (Scotland) Order 1992. The exercise of this permission is subject to a prior approval requirement enabling the planning authority to have the opportunity to control its siting, design and external appearance (Class 22(3)(a) of the Town and Country Planning (General Permitted Development) (Scotland) Amendment Order 1992 and Amendment (No 3) Order 1994).

THE USE CLASSES ORDER

Section 26(2)(f) enables changes of use by way of a Use Classes Order (UCO) issued by Scottish Ministers (Town and Country Planning (Use Classes) (Scotland) Order 1997, as amended), thereby expressly excluding certain changes of use from constituting development. The purpose of the UCO is to group various uses within classes. Any change within these classes does not require planning permission, as such a change of use does not constitute development. The uses set out in the various classes are not intended to be comprehensive. Furthermore, art 3(5) of the UCO makes it clear that no class includes any uses set out in that provision. This includes, *inter alia*, uses which have the potential to affect amenity and includes use for the sale of fuel for motor vehicles (art 3(5)(c)), use as a public house (art 3(5)(h)) and use for the sale of hot food for consumption off the premises (art 3(5)(j)). Such uses are regarded as *sui generis* (in a class of their own).

The schedule to the 1997 Order sets out the classes as follows:

- Class 1: Shops;
- Class 2: Financial, professional and other services;
- Class 3: Food and drink;
- Class 4: Business;

- Class 5: General industrial;
- Class 6: Storage and distribution;
- Class 7: Hotels and hostels;
- Class 8: Residential institutions;
- Class 9: Houses;
- Class 10: Non-residential institutions;
- Class 11: Assembly and leisure.

A change of use from a post office to hairdressers does not require planning permission because it does not constitute development – both uses are within Class 1: shops. A change of use from a post office to a betting shop, however, would require planning permission, as a post office is within Class 1: shops and a betting shop is categorised as Class 2: financial, professional and other services. Change of use from a restaurant, which is included in Class 3: food and drink, to a take away fish and chip shop, would also require planning permission because Class 3 does not include use for the sale of hot food for consumption off the premises, which is categorised as *sui generis*. Part 3 of the Town and Country Planning (General Permitted Development) (Scotland) Order 1992 (as amended) also enables some minor changes of use to take place without requiring planning permission: for example, from Class 3: food and drink to Class 2: financial, professional and other services. This is because a general permission has been granted by way of a statutory instrument. This is considered next.

GENERAL PERMITTED DEVELOPMENT ORDER

Scottish Ministers can make a development order which grants planning permission for certain classes of development (1997 Act, s 31). The granting of planning permission in this way, often referred to as permitted development rights (PDR), removes the need to apply for planning permission, provided the development complies with certain restrictions and conditions set out in the order. It is, however, a matter of fact and degree in the circumstances of each proposal. A general planning permission is given for specified classes of development and this is currently contained within the Town and Country Planning (General Permitted Development) (Scotland) Order 1992 (as amended) (GPDO). The provisions of Sch 1 set out the development that is permitted. The legislation, however, restricts the size, location and other matters relating to that development. If the development falls within the tolerances, as set out in the Order, it is a PDR development and express planning permission is not required because it has been granted by Scottish Ministers.

The most commonly used category is contained in Pt 1: the enlargement, improvement or other alteration of a dwelling house. There are 25 parts to the Order, which include matters such as construction of a fence (Pt 2); industrial and warehouse development (Pt 8); development by statutory undertakers (Pt 13); coal mining (Pt 17); telecommunications development (Pts 20 and 21); and closed circuit television cameras (Pt 25). Recent alterations to the system have included amendments to the GPDO to enable more microgeneration equipment to be installed on existing domestic buildings without the need to apply for planning permission (Town and Country Planning (General Permitted Development) (Domestic Microgeneration) (Scotland) Amendment Orders 2009 and 2010). Article 4 Directions enable Scottish Ministers to restrict PDRs in certain areas: eg conservation areas. Planning permission would therefore be required before development could take place (art 4 of the Town and Country Planning (General Permitted Development) (Scotland) Order 1992, as amended).

IS PLANNING PERMISSION REQUIRED?

In assessing whether planning permission is required there are therefore three preliminary questions to answer:

- Does the proposal fall within the statutory definition of development? If so:
- Is it an activity not considered "development", eg because of the Use Classes Order? If so:
- Are the proposals covered by an existing general planning permission, eg by the GPDO?

If the answer to the second and third questions is no, then a specific planning permission is required for the development. If this is the case, it must then be considered – does the proposal involve both operations and change of use? If so, it will be necessary to include both parts in the application for planning permission.

REFORM OF THE PERMITTED DEVELOPMENT SYSTEM

An extension of the number of uses and building operations that fall into the permitted development regime in Scotland was highlighted in the White Paper, *Modernising the Planning System* (2005), pp 18–20. The new system will replace the existing permitted development (PDR) rights for householder development contained in the Town and Country Planning (General Permitted Development) (Scotland) Order 1992. "This will allow individuals more freedom to develop their property and planning authorities to allocate resources to more significant developments, while retaining an appropriate level of planning control" (Scottish Government, *Householder Permitted Development Rights*, Consultation Paper (December 2008), para 1.2). It is considered that the decrease in workload will help free up staff resources for other planning matters and also help improve efficiency in processing applications overall (*Householder Permitted Development Rights*, Consultation Paper (2008), para 5.7). Research commissioned by the Scottish Government in 2006 recommended changes to permitted development rights that would allow some 38 per cent of householder applications to be removed from the planning application regime – almost 10,000 applications based on the figures for 2006/07. Nevertheless, this element of the reform of the Scottish planning system has proved controversial and has therefore been prolonged (*Analysis of Householder Permitted Development Rights, Consultation Responses* (2009)). It had originally been anticipated that the PDR reforms would have been implemented by 2009. However, at the time of writing, the Scottish Government is arranging focused consultation and negotiation with user groups, with revised legislation and guidance now expected late 2010. When implemented, however, it will complete the planning hierarchy.

The preceding sections have highlighted the intricacies of ascertaining whether planning permission is required for a development. In order to obtain a definite answer, procedures exist within the planning Acts to obtain a formal determination from the planning authority, either in advance of the development or following its completion.

DETERMINING WHETHER PLANNING PERMISSION IS REQUIRED: CERTIFICATES OF LAWFULNESS OF USE OR DEVELOPMENT

A determination as to whether planning permission is required can be given in the form of a Certificate of Lawfulness of Proposed Use or Development (CLOPUD) (1997 Act, s 150). A Certificate of Lawfulness of Existing Use or Development (CLEUD) (1997 Act, s 151) can also be provided, which is a determination of the lawfulness of either any existing use of land or building, or any operations which have been carried out, or any failure to comply with a condition or limitation attached to a grant of planning permission. The introduction of this certificate in 1992 enabled a statutory document to be obtained certifying the lawfulness of existing operational development or use as a single dwelling house for the first time. Prior to this, an application could be made under s 51 of the Town and Country Planning (Scotland) Act 1972 for an Established Use Certificate. Certificates granted prior to 26 September 1992 remain valid.

A CLOPUD or a CLEUD will be issued if the planning authority is satisfied that the use or operations would be lawful if begun at the time of the application. A use or operation is lawful if it is immune from enforcement action and is not in contravention of the requirements of any enforcement notice which is in force. Once the lawfulness of a use or operation has been certified, that use or operation enjoys the permitted development rights conferred by the GPDO.

Any person may apply to the planning authority for a CLOPUD or a CLEUD. The onus is on the applicant to provide sufficient information of the lawfulness to satisfy the planning authority, but not to prove the lawfulness beyond reasonable doubt, and corroboration of the applicant's evidence does not appear to be required (Collar, *Planning* at para 4.56). If sufficient information is provided, the authority will issue a certificate that shall conclusively presume the lawfulness of any use, operation or other matters specified in the certificate. A refusal to issue a certificate, however, is not conclusive evidence that the use or the development is unlawful and will not preclude a future application based on new evidence.

The planning authority may revoke a certificate without compensation if a statement was made or a document used which was false in a material particular or any other information was withheld. The applicant has a right of appeal to Scottish Ministers against a refusal or part refusal to issue a certificate. There is also a right of appeal against a failure to determine an application within the 2-month time limit (1997 Act, s 154(1)(b)). The decision of Scottish Ministers on appeal may be challenged in the Court of Session. Such a challenge is limited to allegations that they acted illegally and the decision on the facts is final.

The certificates are a useful mechanism for clarifying the status of a development, for both developer and the planning authority. They are linked to the enforcement regime (for more detail, see Chapter 11 below).

If a development proposal is exempt from requiring planning permission, there may be other consents to be obtained before development can go ahead, which go beyond the scope of this text. In many cases, however, planning permission is required and this is considered in Chapter 6.

This chapter concludes by outlining two mechanisms introduced in the 1980s to stimulate economic development, which, although currently out of fashion, remain on the statute book. It also considers an approach introduced by the 2006 Act reforms to formalise funding in town centres.

ENTERPRISE ZONES

Enterprise Zones (EZ) were introduced by the Local Government, Planning and Land Act 1980 (now incorporated as s 2 of the 1997 Act), as an experimental initiative to encourage economic development by removing planning controls and providing tax relief. Five were designated in Scotland, but with a lifespan of 10 years; only one is still in force, in Lanarkshire. Planning permission was granted in advance for specified developments within the EZ and it typically provided office development on sites no longer required for industrial development.

SIMPLIFIED PLANNING ZONES

A simplified planning zone (SPZ) is similar, but does not have the taxation advantages associated with EZ. Planning permission was granted in advance through the SPZ scheme, similar to the permitted development regime. They were introduced in 1986 (now incorporated as ss 49–55 of and Sch 5 to the 1997 Act) and all planning authorities were required to consider whether it was desirable for SPZ schemes to be designated for their area and, having done so, to keep the issue under review. There was considerable government encouragement for these schemes, particularly prior to 1997; however, they did not prove popular with planning authorities in Scotland and very few were implemented.

BUSINESS IMPROVEMENT DISTRICTS

A Business Improvement District is a partnership agreement between a local authority and local businesses. Its purpose is to provide better and more integrated town centre services, in order to improve the business environment. There are numerous examples of BIDs in the United States of America and Canada, and such an approach has been adopted by many post industrial cities worldwide. In Scotland, the BID regime was given statutory effect by Pt 9 of the 2006 Act and is incorporated as ss 33–49 of the 1997 Act. It came into force in

April 2007. The Act provides a framework for the establishment of the BIDs, supplemented by the Planning etc (Scotland) Act 2006 (Business Improvement Districts Levy) Order 2007; Business Improvement Districts (Scotland) Regulations 2007; Business Improvement Districts (Ballot Arrangements) (Scotland) Regulations 2007; and Business Improvement Districts (Scotland) (Amendment) Regulations 2008.

To date, nine BIDs have been established in Scotland, with a further ten in development. The process seems to have found favour with both businesses and local government and certainly is more equitable than the previous voluntary system of funding town centre management projects. It is, however, early days for the system in Scotland; although in general terms there are some critics of the BIDs regime, it at least provides "a realistic prospect of enabling city centres to become more attractive and successful, helping businesses and communities" (Scottish Executive, *Building Better Cities – Delivering Growth and Opportunities* (2003)).

Essential Facts

- Planning permission is required for development (1997 Act, s 28(1)).
- Only development that falls within the definition of "development" in s 26(1) of the 1997 Act requires planning permission.
- The definition divides development into "operations" and "material change of use".
- There are some important exclusions from the definition of "development", including the use of land for agriculture and forestry (1997 Act, s 26(2)(e)).
- The Town and Country Planning (Use Classes) (Scotland) Order 1992 (UCO) classifies certain uses together and provides for change of use within these classes without requiring planning permission.
- The Town and Country Planning (General Permitted Development) (Scotland) Order 1992 (GPDO) grants a general planning permission for some forms of development. This is known as "permitted development".
- The White Paper *Modernising the Planning System* (2005) proposed to increase the amount of permitted development – in particular household permitted development. This will form the bottom layer of the planning hierarchy and will be known as "minor development".

- To determine whether planning permission is required the following three questions must be answered:
  - Does the proposal fit the statutory definition of "development"?
  - Is it excluded from development (eg UCO)?
  - Is it covered by a general permission (eg GPDO)?
  If the answers are: "yes", "no" and "no" then a planning application is required.
- A certificate of lawfulness of existing use or development and a certificate of lawfulness of proposed use or development can be obtained from the planning authority.

Essential Cases

Parkes v Secretary of State for the Environment (1978): a proposal for development can fall into both parts of the definition of "development", but only one of the two elements needs to be present in order to be caught by the definition.

Burdle v Secretary of State for the Environment (1972): establishing the planning unit is essential to establish whether a change of use has taken place and, in general, the larger the planning unit, the less likely that a change of use has taken place.

6 PLANNING APPLICATIONS

If a proposed development requires planning permission, a planning application must be submitted to the planning authority in which the development site is located. The process of considering planning applications used to be known as development control. The less adversarial term of development management was included in the White Paper *Modernising the Planning System* (2005), as part of the culture change initiatives for the planning regime in Scotland (p 14). The phrase has now been widely adopted by planning authorities.

Many changes to the planning application procedure were introduced by the 2006 Act reforms. The changes to the development management regime are intended to ensure that procedures for applying for planning permission are fit for purpose and responsive to the different types of development proposals submitted to planning authorities; that they improve efficiency in developing and determining applications, as well as enhancing community involvement at appropriate points in the planning process (Planning Circular 4/2009: *Development Management Procedures*, para 1.3). The most important initiatives are:

- introduction of a hierarchy of developments;
- extensive statutory pre-application requirements;
- planning authorities have responsibility for neighbour notification;
- planning permission in principle replaces outline planning permission.

This chapter covers these reforms in an overall outline of the law relating to the submission of planning applications in Scotland.

HIERARCHY OF DEVELOPMENTS

The hierarchy of developments is at the heart of the modernised planning system in Scotland (Circular 5/2009: *Hierarchy of Developments*, para 1). Rowan Robinson considers this to be the most radical and far-reaching change (*The Town and Country Planning (Scotland) Act 1997* (Green's Annotated Acts, 2009), p xiv). A new s 26A has been added to the 1997 Act, which provides that a development which requires planning permission is to be allocated to one of three categories. Its purpose is to ensure that applications are dealt with in a manner proportionate to their scale and complexity and to allow decisions to be taken at the most appropriate level (Circular 5/2009, para 2). Section 26A identifies three categories in the hierarchy of development to which all developments will be allocated:

- national developments
- major developments
- local developments.

These are illustrated in the diagram below. The fourth and bottom category is that of minor or permitted development and, therefore, does not require planning permission (see Chapter 5).

Hierarchy of development

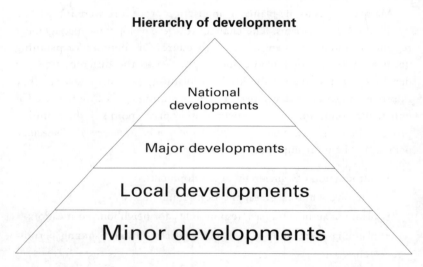

National developments

National developments are at the peak of the hierarchy triangle and are set out in the National Planning Framework (NPF). Section 3A(4)(b) of the 1997 Act provides that the NPF may describe a development and designate it, or a class of development and designate each such development, as a "national" development. The NPF must contain a statement by the Scottish Ministers of their reasons for considering that there is a need for the national development in question (1997 Act, s 3A(5)(a)). It may also contain a statement by the Scottish Ministers as regards other matters pertaining to that designation (1997 Act, s 3A(5)(b)). The importance of this for development management decisions has been highlighted by

Rowan Robinson, who states that the new s 25 (of the 1997 Act) provides that if a development is a national development, the determination by the planning authority must be made in accordance with any statement issued by Scottish Ministers relating to that development, which is expressed to be for the purposes of development management and is to the effect that the development could and should occur (Rowan Robinson, *The Town and Country Planning (Scotland) Act 1997*, pp xv–xvi). NPF2 was approved on 25 June 2009 and identified 14 national developments. It must be reviewed every 5 years and further national developments may be identified at that time (1997 Act, ss 7–9). Planning applications for national developments will be determined by the planning committee of the relevant local authority to which they have been submitted.

Major developments

"Major" developments comprise a range of developments which are significant in scale and will therefore be identified in development plans as such. Nine classes of major development have been defined by the Town and Country Planning (Hierarchy of Developments) (Scotland) Regulations 2009, with thresholds and other relevant criteria set out in Sch 1 to the Regulations. These are as follows:

(1) *EIA Schedule 1 development*: any development of a description mentioned in Sch 1 to the Environmental Impact Assessment (Scotland) Regulations 1999;

(2) *housing*: housing developments where the development comprises 50 or more dwellings or the area of the site exceeds 2 hectares;

(3) *business and general industry, storage and distribution*: business and general industry, storage and distribution where the gross floor area of the building, structure or other erection is or exceeds 10,000m squared or the area of the site is or exceeds 2 hectares;

(4) *electricity generation*: electricity generation where the capacity of the generating station is or exceeds 20 megawatts;

(5) *waste management facilities*: waste management facilities where the capacity of the facility is or exceeds 25,000 tonnes per annum or in relation to facilities for use for the purpose of sludge treatment, a capacity to treat more than 50 tonnes (wet weight) per day of residual sludge;

(6) *transport and infrastructure projects*: transport and infrastructure projects where the length of the road, railway, tramway, waterway, aqueduct or pipeline exceeds 8 kilometres;

(7) *fish farming*: fish farming where the surface area of water covered is or exceeds 2 hectares;

(8) *minerals*: extraction of minerals where the area of the site is or exceeds 2 hectares; and

(9) *other development*: any development not falling wholly within any single class of development described in (1) to (8) above, where the gross floor space of any building, structure or erection constructed as a result of such development is or exceeds 5,000 square metres; or the area of the site is or exceeds 2 hectares.

Planning applications for major developments will be determined by the planning committee of the relevant local authority to which they have been submitted.

Local developments

"Local" developments are all developments other than "national" developments or "major" developments (Town and Country Planning (Hierarchy of Developments) (Scotland) Regulations 2009, reg 2(2)). Scottish Ministers, however, have a general power under s 26A(3) of the 1997 Act to direct that a particular local development should be dealt with as if it were a major development and Scottish Ministers would issue a direction to that effect to the relevant planning authority. It is possible for applications for local developments to be determined by the planning committee of the local authority to whom they are submitted. It was highlighted in the White Paper, *Modernising the Planning System* (2005), however, that many local developments could be most effectively considered through delegated powers (pp 18–20). Section 43A of the 1997 Act, therefore, introduces a new additional scheme of delegation for local developments.

Local developments: schemes of delegation

The ethos of planning decision-making as envisaged in the 1947 legislation was that decisions were made on behalf of the people, by their elected representatives, sitting as a planning committee. The Local Government (Scotland) Act 1973 enabled some decisions to be taken by officers through a scheme of delegation (1973 Act, s 56). The White Paper *Modernising the Planning System* acknowledged that delegation to officers operated successfully in most planning authorities and was an efficient way to deal with many planning applications (p 32). The White Paper, however, proposed that planning authorities provide new delegation schemes, to allow officers to determine a wider range of applications and to be able to make the full range of possible decisions (p 24). Section 43A of the 1997 Act, therefore, introduces a new additional scheme for local developments to run alongside the 1973 scheme.

Planning Circular 7/2009: *Schemes of Delegation and Local Reviews* made it clear that Scottish Ministers wish to encourage planning authorities to make the most effective use of their powers by delegating decision-making on straightforward planning applications to officers, in order that elected members can focus on the more complex or controversial applications (para 7). The new delegation agreement cannot delegate determination of an application for planning permission only in the following three instances (Town and Country Planning (Schemes of Delegation and Local Review Procedure) (Scotland) Regulations 2008, reg 3(4)):

- it is made by a planning authority or by a member of the planning authority;
- it relates to land in the ownership of the planning authority; or
- it relates to land in which the planning authority has a financial interest.

Each planning authority produced a new scheme of delegation by 30 June 2009 and submitted it for approval to Scottish Ministers. The schemes have been operational since 3 August 2009 and applied to applications already in the system, as well as new ones. Research has revealed wide variances across Scotland in the schemes. For example, the number of objections required to take an application for planning permission outwith an officer's power to determine, varied from three to ten. Furthermore, only three local authorities chose maximum delegation, as they imposed no further restrictions on delegation beyond the requirements of the 2008 Regulations. (Brodies LLP, *The new schemes of delegation: Are they promoting efficient decision-making for planning applications in Scotland?* (2010).) Approval by Scottish Ministers, prior to adoption is a new requirement in relation to the 2009 schemes of delegation. All these schemes must be reviewed at least every 5 years (Town and Country Planning (Schemes of Delegation and Local Review Procedure) (Scotland) Regulations 2008, reg 6). One of the most important aspects of this new regime is that the right of appeal to Scottish Ministers under s 47 of the 1997 Act has been removed for applications made or deemed to have been made under the new schemes of delegation. Instead, where an application is determined by an officer, under the scheme of delegation, and is refused or is granted subject to conditions or is not determined within such period as may be prescribed, the applicant may require the planning authority to review the case. This is known as local review (1997 Act, s 43A(8)). (See Chapter 12 below for more details.)

Minor development

Minor development is development that does not require planning permission because a general planning permission has been granted by the General Permitted Development Order. An extension of the number of uses and building operations that fall into this category was highlighted in the White Paper *Modernising the Planning System* (2005) (pp 18–20). Notwithstanding an extensive consultation exercise (*Householder Permitted Development Rights, Consultation Paper* (December 2008) and *Analysis of Householder Permitted Development Rights, Consultation Responses* (December 2009)), the process has yet to be completed and has proved controversial. When implemented, however, it will complete the planning hierarchy. (See Chapter 5 above for more details.)

The hierarchy of developments therefore enables planning applications in the different categories to be dealt with in different ways. National and major developments have more onerous requirements than local developments. Minor developments do not require a planning application. The procedures for each type of planning application are now considered.

NATIONAL AND MAJOR APPLICATIONS: STATUTORY PRE-APPLICATION PROCEDURES

The main changes to the pre-application procedures are relevant only to national and major applications. They relate to pre-application consultation requirements, pre-application discussion, design and access statements and environmental assessment.

Pre-application consultation

Pre-application consultation (PAC) is a new statutory requirement for national and major planning applications (1997 Act, ss 35A–35C). The White Paper *Modernising the Planning System* (2005) noted that, on some occasions, applicants would voluntarily consult with local communities prior to the submission of a planning application and considered that this could be extended to a statutory requirement in appropriate cases (p 36). It is intended to improve the quality of proposals by allowing applicants the opportunity to amend their emerging proposals to accommodate community opinion. It does not take away the right of individuals or communities to express formal views during the planning process, nor does it remove the need for people who wish their views to be considered to make formal representations on the proposals to the planning authority. It became effective from 4 April 2009.

In most cases it will be clear from the definition of major and national developments whether a PAC is required. A screening process, however, enables prospective applicants to seek the planning authority's view, by way of a pre-application notice, as to whether a proposal is a national or a major development and, therefore, requires a PAC (1997 Act, s 35A).

There are three parts to PAC and each is now considered.

Proposal of application notice

A prospective applicant must provide a proposal of application notice to the planning authority at least 12 weeks prior to the submission of an application for planning permission. The requirements of the notice include a description of the development, the postal address, a plan, contact details for the prospective applicant and an account of the consultation processes for the proposal (Town and Country Planning (Development Management Procedure) (Scotland) Regulations 2008, reg 6). The planning authority must respond within 21 days, indicating any additional notification and consultation they require (Circular 4/2009, para 2.13). These must be proportionate, specific and reasonable in the circumstances (Circular 4/2009, para 2.15). General advice on how to conduct this public participation exercise is set out in Planning Advice Note 81: *Community Engagement* (2008).

Minimum consultation activity

The minimum consultation activity for a PAC consists of two elements: formal consultation with community councils and at least one public event. First, every community council, any part of whose area is within or adjoins the land on which the proposed development is situated, must be consulted and the proposal of application notice must be served on them (Town and Country Planning (Development Management Procedure) (Scotland) Regulations 2008, reg 7). Second, at least one public event must be held at which members of the public can make comments on the proposals. The onus for the pre-application consultation is on the prospective applicants and it is not the intention that planning authorities will routinely have a direct role in PAC activities, beyond their statutory roles. The circular advises that "prospective applicants will gain less from poorly attended or unrepresentative PAC events ... applicants should ensure that processes are put in place that will allow members of the community to participate meaningfully in any public event" (Circular 4/2009, para 2.23).

Pre-application consultation reports

The applicant must prepare a report setting out what has been done during the 12-week pre-application process phase, both to comply with the statutory requirements for PAC, as well as any other requirements set out in the planning authority's response to the proposal of application notice (1997 Act, ss 35C and 39). The legislation does not specify the content of the report, but minimum requirements are set out in Circular 4/2009. The report must accompany an application for planning permission, planning permission in principle or a further application under regs 9–11 of the Town and Country Planning (Development Management Procedure) (Scotland) Regulations 2008 and the authority will be required to include it along with the application, plans and drawings. Planning authorities, however, must decline to determine an application where compliance with the PAC requirements has not been demonstrated (1997 Act, s 39(1)(a)).

Pre-application discussions

Pre-application discussions have often formed part of the planning application process. Such informal approaches have usually been welcomed by planning authorities. This is set to continue under the 2006 Act reforms, although with the advent of PAC many local authorities have formalised their procedures. Circular 4/2009, however, makes it clear that there is a distinction between pre-application consultation and pre-application discussion. The pre-application discussion, however, is regarded as an appropriate point to conclude the terms of a processing agreement. (See Chapter 7 below for more details.)

It is the view of Scottish Ministers that both the process of pre-application consultation with the community and that of pre-application discussions with the planning authority are intended to add value at the start of the development management process. They are regarded as a way of improving the quality of the proposals and providing the opportunity to amend emerging proposals in the light of reaction and feedback.

Design and access statements

All applications for planning permission for national and major developments require design and access statements (Town and Country Planning (Development Management Procedure) (Scotland) Regulations 2008, reg 13), which explain:

- the design principles and concepts that have been applied to the development;

- how issues relating to access for disabled people to the development have been dealt with.

Such a statement may relate to either design or access or both.

Design statement

A design statement is required by reg 13(2) of the Town and Country Planning (Development Management Procedure) (Scotland) Regulations 2008 to accompany a planning application in the following circumstances:

- World Heritage Site;
- a conservation area;
- a historic garden or designated landscape;
- a National Scenic Area;
- the site of a scheduled monument; and
- the curtilage of a category A listed building.

A design statement is not required where the development in question comprises the alteration or an extension of an existing building (reg 13(3)), nor for non-compliance with conditions subject to which a previous planning permission was granted (reg 13(3)(a)), nor where it is an application for planning permission for:

- engineering or mining operations;
- development of an existing dwelling house, or development within the curtilage of such a dwelling house for any purpose incidental to the enjoyment of the dwelling house as such; or
- a material change in the use of land or buildings (reg 13(3)(b)).

The main aim of the design statement is to inform the planning decision-making process. It is a written statement which should explain the policy or approach adopted for the design and how any policies relating to design in the development plan have been taken into account. It should also state what, if any, consultation has been undertaken on issues relating to the design principles and what account has been taken of the outcome of any such consultation (reg 13(4)).

Design and access statement

A design and access statement, which should accompany all national and major developments, is a document containing both a design statement and a written statement about how issues relating to access to the development for disabled people have been considered. It should explain the policy or approach adopted and, in particular:

- how policies relating to such access in the development plan have been taken into account;
- how any specific issues which might affect access to the development for disabled people have been addressed;
- describes how features which ensure access to the development for disabled people will be maintained; and
- states what, if any, consultation has been undertaken on issues relating to access to the development for disabled people and what account has been taken of the outcome of any such consultation (reg 13(5)).

Design and access statements are an additional requirement to accompany many planning applications from 3 August 2009. Guidance is provided in *Designing Places,* Planning Advice Note (PAN) 68: *Design Statements* and PAN 78: *Inclusive Design*. Individual planning authorities may also provide advice as to what they will require in these statements.

Environmental assessment

Environmental assessment has developed internationally as a key environmental law mechanism. It now encompasses both Environmental Impact Assessment (EIA) and Strategic Environmental Assessment (SEA) and their use extends beyond that of the planning regime. Throughout the United Kingdom, however, EIA is closely associated with the planning application process, which is considered in this chapter. (See Chapter 4 for more detail on SEA.) European law requires specified public and private projects to have an assessment of their environmental effects before the development consent is granted (EEC Directive 85/337 as amended by Directive 97/11). This process is known as Environmental Impact Assessment (EIA). It is implemented in Scotland by the Town and Country Planning (Environmental Impact Assessment) (Scotland) Regulations 1999. The legislation is supported by Circular 8/2007: *The Environmental Impact Assessment (Scotland) Regulations 1999.* The regulations have been amended several times, most recently by the Environmental Impact Assessment (Scotland) Amendment Regulations 2009, in order to accommodate the 2006 Act reforms. At the time of writing, however, the Scottish Government is undertaking a consultation on consolidating and updating Pt II of the Environmental Impact Assessment (Scotland) Regulations 1999 and it is anticipated that these changes will be implemented later in 2010. The consultation paper notes that the European Commission has recently undertaken its own review of the application and effectiveness of the EIA Directive, and, therefore, changes in the whole process at a European-wide level may be anticipated in due course.

Environmental Impact Assessment (EIA)

EIA (like SEA) is both a technique and a process. Bell and McGillivray observe that "strictly, the 'assessment' is undertaken by the decision maker, on the basis of environmental information with which it is supplied" (*Environmental Law* (7th edn, 2008), p 432). In the context of this chapter, it is therefore the planning authority or Scottish Ministers who undertake the assessment as part of the planning decision-making process, on the basis of the environmental information supplied as an environmental statement, as part of the planning application submission.

It is the nature of the proposal that instigates the process of EIA and lists are set out in Schs 1 and 2 to the 1999 Regulations. An environmental statement is always necessary for development falling within Sch 1, which incorporates Annex 1 to the Directive and contains detailed criteria. The list includes development types that would clearly be regarded as having an impact on the environment. For example: crude oil refineries, nuclear power stations, long distance railway lines, airports and major roads; waste disposal installations for the incineration, chemical treatment or landfill of hazardous and non-hazardous waste; and installations for the storage of petroleum, petrochemical or chemical products with a capacity of 200,000 tonnes or more.

Proposals which fall into Sch 2 may require an EIA. An extensive list is provided with tolerances which trigger the need for an EIA. For example: use of uncultivated land for intensive agriculture (exceeding 0.5 hectare); industrial installations for electricity, steam, and hot water production, other than Sch 1 (exceeding 0.5 hectare); developments in the chemical industry where new floor space exceeds 1,000 square metres of new floor space; permanent racing and test tracks for motorised vehicles (exceeding 1 hectare) and skiing-related developments (exceeding 1 hectare or a building exceeding 15 metres).

The planning authority may "screen" applications for Sch 2 developments, to determine whether an environmental statement is required. The screening opinion can also be sought by the local authority if a developer is uncertain whether the proposed development is EIA development (reg 5 of the 1999 Regulations). Schedule 3 to the Regulations contains selection criteria for screening, to assist in the determination as to whether an environmental statement is required. These include characteristics of the development (eg its size), the use of natural resources, the location of the development and the characteristics of the potential impact. Scottish Ministers may issue a screening direction (reg 6). Scottish Ministers also have the power to apply EIA to additional classes of development beyond those classes already specified in Directives 85/337/EEC and 97/11/EC (1997 Act, s 40(1)). Circular 8/2007 sets out in detail the process for establishing whether an EIA is required (paras 27–86).

It is the applicant's responsibility to prepare the environmental statement. There is no statutory provision as to its form. It may consist of one or more documents, but it must constitute a "single and accessible compilation" (*Berkeley* v *Secretary of State for the Environment, Transport and the Regions and Fulham Football Club* (*No 1*) (2001)). It must contain the information specified in Pt II and such of the relevant information in Pt I of Sch 4 to the 1999 Regulations as is reasonably required to assess the effects of the project and which the applicant can reasonably be required to compile (reg 2(1)). Paragraph 87 of Circular 8/2007 explains that whilst every environmental statement should provide a full factual description of the development, the emphasis of Sch 4 is on the "main" or "significant" environmental effects to which development is likely to give rise. Where significant adverse effects are identified, the statement must contain a description of the remedial measures which the developer proposes.

The list of aspects of the environment which might significantly be affected by a project is set out in para 3 of Pt I of Sch 4. It includes:

- human beings;
- flora;
- fauna;
- soil;
- water;
- air;
- climate;
- landscape;
- material assets;
- any architectural or archaeological heritage;
- the interaction of any of the above.

Consideration should also be given to the likely significant effects resulting from the use of:

- natural resources;
- the emission of pollutants;

- the creation of nuisances;
- the elimination of waste.

In addition to the direct effects of a development, the environmental statement should also cover the following types of effects:

- indirect;
- secondary;
- cumulative;
- short, medium and long term;
- permanent;
- temporary;
- positive and negative.

Circular 8/2007 notes that these are comprehensive lists and that a particular project may give rise to significant effects in only one or two respects (para 89). The information in the environmental statement must be summarised in a non-technical summary (para 5 of Pt II of Sch 4 to the 1999 Regulations). Circular 8/2007 advises that applicants are encouraged to publish the non-technical summary as a separate document and to make copies available free of charge in order to facilitate wider public consultation (para 110). This can be done before the submission of the planning application to the planning authority.

Advice on the preparation of the environmental statement is provided in Circular 8/2007 and PAN 58: *Environmental Impact Assessment*. In order to prepare the statement, relevant information held by the planning authority and certain consultation bodies should be made available to the applicant (Environmental Information (Scotland) Regulations 2004). The developer will formally notify the planning authority that an environmental statement is being prepared and the planning authority will inform the consultation bodies of the details of the proposed development and that they may be requested to provide relevant non-confidential information.

The consultation bodies are:

- any adjoining planning authority (where the development is likely to affect land in their area);
- Scottish Natural Heritage;
- Scottish Water;
- SEPA;
- the Health and Safety Executive;

- the Scottish Ministers;
- other statutory bodies relevant to a particular application.

The applicants may also seek a formal, but non-binding, opinion from the planning authority about what information should be provided in the environmental statement (reg 10). This is known as "scoping" and allows the developer to be clear about what the planning authority considers the main effects of the development are likely to be, and, therefore, the topics on which the environmental statement should focus (Circular 8/2007, para 94). Where a planning authority fails to adopt a scoping opinion within 5 weeks (or an agreed extension), the developer may apply to Scottish Ministers for a scoping direction (reg 10(7)). An environmental statement, however, is not necessarily invalid if it does not fully comply with the scoping opinion or direction (Circular 8/2007, para 100).

An application for planning permission which requires an environmental statement must be accompanied by the statement at the time of submission of the application to the planning authority. All the documents which would normally accompany a planning application (see below) must be submitted. In addition, the applicant must submit:

- five copies of the statement (three of which are sent to Scottish Ministers);
- the certification required by reg 13(3);
- a note of the name of every body to whom the applicant has already sent a non-technical summary;
- such further copies of the statement as are needed to allow the planning authority to send one to other consultation bodies.

Furthermore, the applicant must make a reasonable number of copies of the environmental statement available to the public, either free of charge or at a reasonable cost. How the environmental statement contributes to the decision-making process is considered in Chapter 7. The general process of submission of planning applications is considered next.

MAKING A PLANNING APPLICATION

A standard national planning application form is anticipated as part of the modernisation of the planning system in Scotland. At the time of writing, however, there was no date for its introduction. Each planning authority has its own form and this must be used to apply for development in its area. Since 1 April 2009, planning applications for any area in Scotland can be submitted online, although many local authorities had e-planning prior to that date. All planning applications and associated documents submitted from 1 April 2009 can be viewed online and accessed through the Scottish Government Planning homepage, as well as the individual planning authority websites.

Types of planning application

The types of planning application and the procedure for submission changed with the implementation of the relevant parts of the 2006 Act and the accompanying secondary legislation on 3 August 2009. The main changes are now contained within Pt III of the 1997 Act and the Town and Country Planning (Development Management Procedure) Regulations 2008. This is supplemented by Circular 4/2009: *Development Management Procedures*, particularly Pt 3: Making a Planning Application, which states that applicants should be encouraged to think beyond the statutory minimum requirements for an application, and try to anticipate, in discussion with the planning authority, what additional information might be needed to support efficient processing of the application (para 3.3).

There are four main types of planning application:

(1) application for planning permission in principle;

(2) application for planning permission;

(3) application for approval of matters specified in conditions;

(4) further applications.

The law and procedure for these types of application are now considered.

Application for planning permission in principle

Planning permission in principle replaces "outline planning permission". It is defined as "planning permission (a) in respect of the carrying out of building, engineering, mining or other operations in, on, over or under land, and (b) subject to a condition that the development in question will not be begun until certain matters (which may, but need not be particularised in the application) have been approved by the planning authority or Scottish Ministers" (1997 Act, s 59(1)(b)). Planning permission in principle can only be granted for operational development, ie it cannot be sought for change of use. Time limits for submission of the subsequent details to enable the development to commence is, in general, 3 years from the grant of the planning permission in principle (1997 Act, s 59(2)).

An application in principle will be used to establish the acceptability of a proposal, without having to develop the detailed proposals. The planning authority can require additional information where it is considered necessary to determine the application (Town and Country Planning (Development Management Procedure) Regulations 2008, reg 24).

Application requirements for planning permission in principle An application for planning permission in principle must contain the following details (Town and Country Planning (Development Management Procedure) (Scotland) Regulations 2008, reg 10):

- a written description outlining the development;
- the postal address of the land to which the development relates, or a description of the location of the land; and
- the name and address of the applicant or agent.

The application must be accompanied by:

- a plan to identify the land and its relationship to the locality and neighbouring land;
- appropriate certificates required under reg 15 in relation to owners and agricultural tenants;
- where access to the site is to be taken directly from a road, a description of the location of the access points to the proposed development;
- where the application relates to development belonging to the categories of national developments or major developments, a pre-application consultation report; and
- the appropriate fee payable under the Fees Regulations, including fees for advertisements.

Application for planning permission

This is the most common type of planning application submission, used when it is intended that all the information necessary to enable the authority to reach its decision is included in one application.

Application requirements for planning permission The requirements for a submission of planning permission are set out by reg 9 of the Town and Country Planning (Development Management Procedure) (Scotland) Regulations 2008 and are as follows:

- a written description outlining the development;
- the postal address of the land to which the development relates, or a description of the location of the land;

- the name and address of the applicant or agent;
- a plan to identify the land and its relationship to the locality and neighbouring land;
- such other plans and drawings as are necessary to describe the development. The plans and drawings submitted must accurately describe the proposals and tie in with the written description of the development. Annex D to Circular 4/2009 describes the main type of plan that is commonly submitted;
- certificates as required under reg 15 in relation to owners and agricultural tenants; and
- the appropriate fee payable under the Fees Regulations, including fees for advertisements.

An application for planning permission may also require to be accompanied by:

- a pre-application consultation report (national or major applications);
- a design statement or a design and access statement as required by reg 13;
- an ICNIRP declaration, if it is for installation of an antenna to be employed in an electronic communication network.

Application for approval of matters specified in conditions imposed on a grant of planning permission in principle

This type of planning permission deals with the details of the application which has previously been approved as planning permission in principle. All the details may be submitted as one application or may be submitted as a series of subsequent applications (1997 Act, s 59(2)).

Application requirements following planning permission in principle The requirements for this type of application are set out in reg 10 of the Town and Country Planning (Development Management Procedure) (Scotland) Regulations 2008. An application for such approval, consent or agreement is to be in writing and must include the following:

- identification of the planning permission to which it relates;
- a description of the matter in respect of which the application is made;
- the name and address of applicant or agent;

- the appropriate fee payable under the Fees Regulations, including fees
  for advertisements.

Where the application relates to the alteration or construction of
buildings, other structures or roads or to landscaping, it must be
accompanied by plans and drawings describing the matter in respect of
which the application is made.

Further applications

The further application category relates to planning applications that are
submitted for a development that already has planning permission and
either another application is submitted before the commencement date
expires (1997 Act, ss 58 and 59) or an application is made to change one
or a number of the conditions associated with the existing permission
(1997 Act, s 42). In such cases only certain requirements on the content
of the applications are applicable (Circular 4/2009, para 3.8). The
requirements for this type of application are set out in reg 11 of the Town
and Country Planning (Development Management Procedure) (Scotland)
Regulations 2008. Any further application for planning permission or
planning permission in principle must be in writing and provide enough
information to allow the planning authority to identify the previous grant
of permission and include:

- the name and address of the applicant or agent;
- certificates as required under reg 15 in relation to owners and agricultural tenants;
- where the application relates to national development or major
  development, a pre-application consultation report;
- the appropriate fee payable under the Fees Regulations, including fees
  for advertisements;
- where the application relates to the relaxation of conditions attached
  to a previous permission under s 42 of the 1997 Act, a statement to
  that effect.

PLANNING APPLICATION FEES

Most planning applications are accompanied by a planning fee (1997 Act,
s 252). The detail is provided by regulations, the principal regulations
being the Town and Country Planning (Fees for Applications and Deemed
Applications) (Scotland) Regulations 2004; the most recent amendment

was made by the Town and Country Planning (Fees for Applications and Deemed Applications) (Scotland) Amendment Regulations 2010, which raised the fees for applications from 1 April 2010. Chapter 7 of the White Paper *Modernising the Planning System* (2005) considered the financial impacts of the reform process. It states that, as with any reform package, "[the] proposals will generate costs and savings. An effective, efficient planning system which is proportionate in its focus, should have a highly beneficial impact on the wider economy" (p 50). It specifically states that raising the level of fees payable to local authorities for major applications will reflect the cost of processing them more closely (p 50).

COMMENT ON PLANNING APPLICATION SUBMISSION PROCESS

The 2006 Act reforms have made many changes to the processes for submitting planning applications in Scotland. Although more information may be required at the start, a real attempt has been made at streamlining the process. In particular, the move to a hierarchy of developments enables different procedures to be utilised appropriate for the type of application. This will have consequences throughout the development management system (considered elsewhere in this book).

All planning applications are submitted in the first instance to the local planning authority. This is the local authority, except in the Loch Lomond and the Trossachs national park area, where the Park Authority is the planning authority. The decision on the planning application will also, in most cases, be made by the authority to which it is submitted. For some applications, however, the application is called in for determination. This can occur in the Cairngorms National Park within the Cairngorms national park area. It can also occur for any application that raises issues of national significance, which can then be called in for determination by Scottish Ministers. This call-in process is considered as part of the next chapter.

Essential Facts

- If planning permission is required, a planning application must be submitted to the local authority for the area in which the development is located.

Hierarchy of development

- There is a hierarchy of development: national, major and local (1997 Act, s 26A).
- National developments are identified in the NPF.
- Major developments are defined by the Town and Country Planning (Hierarchy of Developments) (Scotland) Regulations 1999.
- National and major developments have statutory pre-application consultation (1997 Act, ss 35A–35C) and the requirement to submit design and access statements (Town and Country Planning (Development Management Procedure) (Scotland) Regulations 2008, reg 13).
- Local developments are all other planning applications and will be dealt with mostly through delegated powers (1997 Act, s 43A and Circular 7/2009: *Schemes of Delegation and Local Review*).

Types of planning application

- There are four main types of planning application (Town and Country Planning (Development Management Procedure) (Scotland) Regulations 2008, regs 9–12):
  - application for planning permission in principle;
  - application for planning permission;
  - application for approval of reserved matters;
  - further applications.

Environmental impact assessment

- Many applications will require environmental impact assessment (EEC Directives 85/337 and 97/11).
- The criteria are set out in Schs 1 and 2 to the Environmental Impact Assessment (Scotland) Regulations 1999.
- Such applications require to be accompanied by an environmental statement.

7 MAKING THE DECISION

Scottish planning authorities now deal with an average of 50,000 planning applications a year (54,597 in 2006–07 and 47,220 in 2008–09). How the decision on each of these planning applications is made is the crux of the planning system. The determination of planning applications is the tool for implementation of planning policy. Each planning application, however, is considered on its own merits and the role of the development plan and "material considerations" is important. The process is a complex combination of procedural requirements within the framework of law and policy.

The process of making the planning decision has changed significantly by virtue of the 2006 Act reforms. This chapter is in two parts. First, it sets out the procedures to be followed upon receipt of planning applications by local authorities. It highlights the different requirements for different types of development, particularly national and major developments. The second part is an examination of the legal requirements for making a decision; it deals with the primacy of the development plan and the role of material considerations.

PROCEDURE UPON RECEIPT OF APPLICATION

The Planning etc (Scotland) Act 2006 changed the name for the process of determining applications from development control to development management (Pt 3 of the 2006 Act, inserted as Pt III of the Town and Country Planning (Scotland) Act 1997). Most local authorities in Scotland have adopted this new title. One of the themes of the reform process was greater certainty and speed of decision-making. Scottish Government policy guidance indicates that development management services should operate within a climate of continuous improvement and processes should be responsive, reliable, transparent and efficient (*Scottish Planning Policy* (2010), para 22). The procedure by planning authorities upon receipt of planning applications is regulated by a range of legislation and secondary instruments, principally the Town and Country Planning (Scotland) Act 1997 (as amended by the Planning etc (Scotland) Act 2006), the Town and Country Planning (General Development Procedures) (Scotland) Regulations 1992 (as amended), the Town and

Country Planning (Development Management Procedure) Regulations 2008 and Circular 4/2009: *Development Management Procedures*. The process undertaken by the planning authority once an application has been submitted is illustrated by the diagram below.

Process for determining a planning application

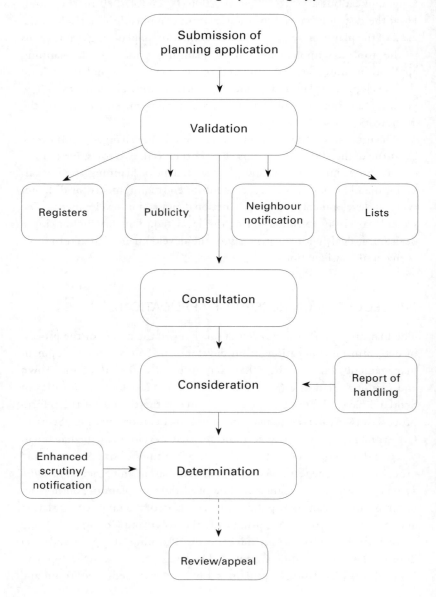

There are ten aspects of procedure specifically set out below:

- checking and validation;
- planning registers and lists;
- neighbour notification;
- publicity;
- consultations;
- environmental impact assessment;
- pre-determination hearing;
- notification;
- processing agreements;
- time limits for decisions.

Each is now considered in turn.

Checking and validation of planning application

On receipt of an application, it is the responsibility of the planning authority to check that the application has been made according to the 2008 Regulations, as follows:

- application for planning permission – reg 9;
- application for planning permission in principle – reg 10;
- further applications – reg 11;
- application for matters specified in conditions – reg 12.

There is no obligation on planning authorities to process applications where there is a failure by the applicant to meet the necessary requirements for submission (Circular 4/2009, para 4.13 and Annex E). (See Chapter 6 for more details.) The planning authority, however, must send a notice detailing the information or documentation that the applicant needs to submit in order to comply with the regulations (reg 17(3)). Once all the correct information is received, the planning authority must acknowledge the application (reg 17(1)). The acknowledgement must include an explanation of the timescales within which the planning authority is to give notice of its decision and indicate the rights of appeal or review on the grounds of non-determination (reg 17(2)). (See Chapter 12 for more details.) Circular 4/2009 indicates that in acknowledging receipt of applications or requesting missing information, planning authorities may request information beyond the statutory minimum required to determine the application (para 4.12). The administrative checking of applications should be carried out as soon as possible and certainly within 5 days of receipt of the application (Circular 4/2009, para 4.4). The planning authority will check the following:

- that the proposal is development as defined by s 26 of the 1997 Act, and therefore requires planning permission;
- the appropriate application forms have been correctly completed and signed;
- the appropriate number and type of plans have been submitted;
- the appropriate certificates have been completed and signed;
- the correct fee has been paid, including any fee for advertising the application;
- any necessary action in respect of site notices has been undertaken;
- any necessary supporting documents have been submitted (eg an environmental statement).

The validation date for applications is the date the last piece of information required by the 2008 Regulations is received (reg 14). Following validation, the application is entered on the statutory register and neighbour notification is undertaken by the planning authority. These are considered next.

Planning register and lists

All valid planning applications must be entered on the statutory register and a weekly list of planning applications produced by the planning authority (1997 Act, s 36). However, the 2006 Act reforms introduced some important changes to planning authorities' obligations in relation to the presentation and content of the planning register. Planning authorities must also provide a list of extant applications accessible to the general public. This list is to be kept in two parts: the first part for applications, the second part for proposal of application notices with respect to requirements for pre-application consultation (reg 21). (See Chapter 6 for more details.)

The planning register records the details of all applications submitted to the planning authority. Since 1 April 2009, all planning authorities in Scotland have had facilities to receive planning applications through the internet and all planning applications forms and plans received since then can be viewed through local authority websites. All local authorities, however, maintain hard copies of plans which can be viewed at their offices. Once a decision has been reached on a planning application, the details will be recorded on the planning register.

Section 36(1) of the 1997 Act requires the registers to be kept in the manner specified in Sch 2 to the 2008 Regulations. Part I contains: a description of the development, details of the applicant and copies of plans and drawings; any design statement or design and access statement; any pre-application consultation report; and particulars of any direction in respect of the application. Part II contains: a copy of the decision notice and copies of the plans considered by the planning authority in determining the application; a copy of any environmental statement; a copy of any appeal decision; and a copy of any review decision. A new requirement is the report of the handling of the application (except for those undergoing a local review). The register also contains information on Certificates of Lawful Use or Development (Sch 2(5) to the 2008 Regulations). Every register is to include an index which is in the form of a map and this is to be kept at the office of the planning authority.

Neighbour notification

An important change introduced as part of the reform of the Scottish planning regime was the move from neighbour notification by the applicants to the planning authority. This was implemented by the Town and Country Planning (Development Management Procedure) Regulations 2008 and Circular 4/2009: *Development Management Procedures*. Neighbour notification is required for applications for planning permission, planning permission in principle and applications for approval of matters specified in conditions attached to a planning permission in principle. The planning authority must give notice that an application has been received by way of a notice, and, where there are premises situated on the neighbouring land, the notice must be sent to the owner, lessee or occupier of such premises. Where there are no such premises, publication of a notice under reg 20 of the 2008 Regulations is required (reg 18(2)). Neighbouring land is defined as "an area or plot of land which or part of which is co-terminous with or within 20 metres of the boundary of the land for which the development is proposed", by reg 3(1) of the Town and Country Planning (Development Management Procedure (Scotland) Regulations 2008, as amended by the Town and Country Planning (Miscellaneous Amendments) (Scotland) Regulations 2009. The requirements for the notice are set out in the 2008 Regulations (reg 18(3)). If there is a failure to notify a notifiable neighbour, a subsequent grant of planning permission may be challenged by way of judicial review (see Chapter 12).

Publicity

There are publicity requirements associated with many planning applications. The Town and Country Planning (Development Management

Procedure) (Scotland) Regulations 2008, reg 20 sets out four circumstances where an application for planning permission or planning permission in principle has been submitted and there are requirements for publicity by the local authority. First, this is required where it is not possible for the planning authority to carry out notification because there are no premises on neighbouring land to which notification can be sent (reg 20(a)). Second, publicity must be undertaken when the applicant has certified under reg 15 that it has not been possible to notify all owners and agricultural tenants of the proposed development (reg 20(b)). Third, there is a requirement for publicity if the application relates to one or more of the classes of development specified in Sch 3 to the 2008 Regulations (reg 20(c)). These are the types of development previously known as "bad neighbour development" and include such works and uses as: the construction of buildings for use as a public convenience (Sch 3(1) to the 2008 Regulations); the construction of buildings or other operations for use of land for the retention, treatment or disposal of sewage, trade waste or effluent (with some exceptions) (Sch 3(2)(b) of the 2008 Regulations); and the construction or use of buildings for a number of uses including a cinema, hot food shop or licensed premises (Sch 3(4) to the 2008 Regulations). Finally, publicity of an application is required if it relates to an application which does not accord with the provisions of the development plan. In these circumstances, the planning authority must publish a notice in the form set out in Sch 4 to the 2008 Regulations, in a newspaper circulating in the locality. The neighbour notification process and the publicity requirements may result in representations being submitted to the planning authority about the proposal. These will contribute to the decision on the application.

Consultations on planning applications

The planning authority will carry out a number of statutory and other consultations and notifications prior to determination of a planning application. Their number and nature will depend on the type of application. Statutory consultation requirements are set out in Sch 5 to and reg 25 of the 2008 Regulations. Planning authorities can undertake such other consultations, in addition to the statutory consultations, as they consider necessary to determine the application. The main consultees, many of which are also key agencies, are discussed in Chapter 2. Scottish Ministers can also direct that planning authorities must consult with other authorities, bodies or persons on a particular application or class of application (reg 25). No less than 14 days' notice is to be given for the consultee to respond (reg 25). If no response is forthcoming in that period, the planning authority is not required to postpone a determination until a response is received. However, the planning authority may wish to consider the potential impact of proceeding in the absence of a consultee's views (Circular 4/2009, para 4.69).

In certain limited cases the consultee will have the power of direction, in which case the planning authority must proceed as directed. In all other cases of consultation, the planning authority must take the consultation response into account, but is not bound by its views. Statutory consultees may also indicate to the planning authority that consultation with them is not required in certain circumstances or in relation to a particular location (reg 25).

Environmental impact assessment

There are particular requirements relating to procedures when an environmental impact assessment (EIA) is involved as part of the decision-making process on a planning application. These include: sending three copies of the environmental statement to Scottish Ministers; placing a copy on the planning register; and undertaking additional consultations (Environmental Impact Assessment (Scotland) Regulations 1999, reg 13). There are also statutory requirements relating to advertisement and publicity of the environmental statement, including where it can be inspected (Environmental Impact Assessment (Scotland) Regulations 1999, reg 19).

The submission of the statement will set in motion publicity and consultation requirements in order to achieve the collection of a range of environmental information, relevant to this particular planning application, which must be taken into account before planning permission is granted. Planning permission cannot be granted unless the procedures have been followed. The statutory period for determining an application with an environmental statement is 4 months (Environmental Impact Assessment (Scotland) Regulations 1999, reg 45). This time period does not begin until the environmental statement has been submitted to the planning authority.

EIA is not intended to be preventive; there is nothing in the legislation that requires refusal of a planning permission because negative environmental impacts are highlighted as part of the environmental assessment process. Nor are conditions required to be attached to a planning permission to mitigate or compensate for such an impact.

Once the application has been determined the planning authority shall:

- inform Scottish Ministers and the consultation authorities;
- inform the public by advertisement or otherwise;
- make a copy of the decision available for public inspection.

The documentation sets out the following:

- the content of the decision and any conditions;
- the main reasons and considerations on which the decision is based;
- a description, where necessary, of the main measures to avoid, reduce and, if possible, offset the major adverse effects of the development.

Pre-determination hearings

Pre-determination hearings must be provided by the planning authority in respect of applications for planning permission and planning permission in principle for major developments where they are significantly contrary to the development plan and in respect of national developments (1997 Act, s 38A). Circular 4/2009 explains that they are part of the enhanced scrutiny measures introduced by the 2006 Act reforms, to make the planning system in Scotland more inclusive (para 4.71). The planning authority must give the applicant and people who submitted representations to it in respect of the application an opportunity of appearing before and being heard by a committee of the authority. This process, in particular, allows neighbours and other members of the public fully to articulate their views on a proposal. The planning authority has discretion over how the hearings operate. This includes ensuring that the matters discussed at a hearing are relevant, efficient and avoid repetition. Attendance beyond those who have a right to appear before and be heard by the committee is to be such as the authority considers appropriate, but guidance is provided in Annex F of Circular 4/2009. Guidance has also been provided as to what constitutes "significant": "where approval would be contrary to the vision or wider spatial strategy of the plan", although there is recognition that this judgement will lie with the planning authority (Circular 4/2009, para 4.75). In cases in which there has been a pre-determination hearing, the application will then be decided by the full council of the local authority (s 14(2) of the Planning etc Scotland Act 2006, amending the Local Government (Scotland) Act 1973). This is a new requirement and has also been introduced to assist with transparency and accountability to the decision-making framework for planning decisions (Circular 4/2009, para 4.67).

Notifications

Scottish Ministers

The Town and Country Planning (Notification of Applications) (Scotland) Direction 2009 sets out the circumstances in which a planning authority proposing to grant an application planning permission requires to notify Scottish Ministers. The Schedule to the Direction sets out the categories of planning applications and circumstances in which planning authorities must notify Scottish Ministers, before they grant planning permission. These are as follows:

(1) Development in which planning authorities have an interest:
  (a) for which the planning authority is the applicant or developer;
  (b) in respect of which the planning authority has a financial or other interest; or
  (c) is to be located on land which is wholly or partly in the planning authority's ownership or in which it has an interest.

(2) Objection by Government Agency relating to:
  (a) development affecting trunk road and special roads;
  (b) development in the vicinity of major hazards;
  (c) nature conservation;
  (d) scheduled monuments and category A listed buildings;
  (e) flooding;
  (f) playing fields;
  (g) marine fish farm developments;

(3) Open cast coal and related minerals.

There are tolerances for (a)–(g) set out in the Schedule to the Direction. This list represents a reduction in the types of application that require to be notified to Scottish Ministers. The revised system is designed to be more proportionate and to apply only to applications which raise issues of national importance (Planning Circular 3/2009: *Notification of Applications*, para 8). In relation to other categories of development, the Scottish Ministers will issue case-specific notification directions to require specific applications to be notified to Scottish Ministers. This will be done only where it appears that there is some matter of national interest involved which requires consideration by Scottish Ministers.

The information to be sent to Scottish Ministers is set out in the 2009 Direction. The effect of notification to Scottish Ministers of intention by a planning authority to approve an application is that it effectively puts a brake on the approval process. The planning authority must not approve the application until 28 days has expired from the date of receipt by Scottish Ministers of all the relevant information on the notified planning application. The Scottish Ministers, within that 28-day period, decide whether to call in the application for their own determination (1997 Act, s 46). Where it takes longer to reach a decision as to whether the application should be called in, Scottish Ministers will issue a further direction to extend their period of consultation. If at the end of the 28-day period, or any extended period, the Scottish Government has not issued a direction or extended the period for consideration, the planning authority can proceed to determine the application (Circular 3/2009, para 28).

Cairngorms National Park

The two national parks in Scotland have differences in relation to their planning powers. (See Chapter 2 for more details.) The Loch Lomond and the Trossachs Park Authority is the planning authority for the area of the Park: it has full planning powers and therefore determines all planning applications.

The Cairngorms National Park Designation, Transitional and Consequential Provisions (Scotland) Order 2003, in designating the national park, limited the Park Authority to sole responsibility for preparing development plans for the park area and shared responsibility with the relevant local authorities (Aberdeenshire, Angus, Highland and Moray Councils) for enforcement and special controls over trees, amenity notices and advertisements. Planning applications within the Cairngorms national park area are therefore submitted in the first instance to the relevant local authority. Planning authorities dealing with planning applications in the Cairngorms national park boundary are under an obligation to pay "special attention" to the desirability of exercising powers consistently with the park plan (1997 Act, s 264A). The Cairngorms Park Authority is notified of all planning applications within the National Park boundary (reg 36(2)). Any application where it appears to the planning authority that development is likely to affect land in the area must also consult the Cairngorms National Park Authority (reg 36(3)). The Park Authority has the power to call in for determination those planning applications which it considers raise issues of general significance for the statutory National Park aims. Once an application has been called in, the Cairngorm National Park Authority becomes the determining authority for that application. There are no powers of delegation and therefore decisions are made at meetings of the Cairngorm Park Authority. The process is similar to that of the planning committees in Scotland prior to delegation being introduced in the 1970s. This is now in stark contrast to the system operated under the 2006 Act reforms, as, since August 2009, relatively few applications are considered by planning committee. The introduction of the hierarchy of developments, with the majority of applications being classified as local developments, means they are being determined by officers under delegated powers. An appeal against a decision of the Cairngorms Park Authority is to Scottish Ministers.

Processing agreements

A processing agreement is an agreed framework for processing an application or related group of planning applications (Circular 4/2009, para 6.1). There is no legislative requirement for processing agreements but it is anticipated that they will be used with major and national developments. It does not guarantee consent, but there are benefits to the system listed at para 6.3 of Circular 4/2009, including greater predictability and certainty over the timing of key stages and effective project management with a focus on delivery. When a processing agreement is in place, however, there is no right of appeal against non-determination until the expiry of the period in the agreement. It is expected that such agreements will be discussed prior to the submission of the planning application; and guidance on the preparation, scope, form and content is set out at paras 6.6–6.11 in Circular 4/2009.

Time limits for decisions

The planning authority has 4 months from the validation date in which to determine applications for national and major applications. It has 2 months to determine local applications and applications for approval, consent or agreement of the planning authority as a consequence of a condition attached to a grant of permission (reg 26). The period for consideration of the application for planning permission may be extended by agreement in writing between the applicant and the planning authority before the right of appeal or review is reached (reg 26).

An application for planning permission, however, is not to be determined until the expiry of the period for making representations in respect of the application has expired. One application may have a number of different time periods associated with it: for example, neighbour notification and an advertisement in local newspapers.

Many of the procedures provide very useful information about the proposal from consultees. The publicity requirements often result in representations either in support of or objecting to the proposed development. These will contribute to the decision-making process on the planning application, and this is considered next.

MAKING THE DECISION

The decision-maker on a planning application will most commonly be the planning authority. Increasingly, following the introduction of the new development management regime from 3 August 2009, this will be the "appointed person" under delegated powers (see Chapter 6). Decisions taken by planning officers avoid the delays inherent in decision-making by elected members at committee, not least because decisions will be made once all the information is available as the determination will not have to await the next planning committee meeting. National and major applications, however, will be determined by a planning committee made up of the elected representatives to the local council and, if such an application has been the subject of a pre-determination hearing, it will require to be considered and decided upon by a meeting of the full Council of the local authority. If the application is in the Cairngorm National Park, it may be called in by the Cairngorm National Park Authority for its determination. Scottish Ministers may also call in certain applications in order that they may make the decision on it. If the application is submitted for review, it will be considered by the Local Review Body; and if it is appealed, a decision will be made by a reporter or by Scottish Ministers. (See Chapter 12 for more details.) In all circumstances, decision-making on planning applications has to follow the legal procedure. This process was summed up by Lord Justice-Clerk Gill, in *Moray Council* v *Scottish Ministers* (2007):

> "[The decision-maker's] starting point will be the development plan;
> considered if need be in the light of national planning guidance. Having
> regard to the development plan framework and the nature of the proposal,
> he must decide what are the determining issues. With those issues in mind,
> he must make his findings in fact on the nature of the proposal and its
> probable effects. It is for him to decide what lines of evidence are material
> to the determining issues and what conclusions are to be drawn from
> them. The [decision-maker] must then decide in the light of his findings
> how he resolves the determining issues. This involves the exercise of his
> planning expertise and judgment."

The decision-making process is governed by two sections of the 1997 Act – ss 25(1) and 37(2). Section 25(1) states: "Where in making any determination under the planning Acts, regard is to be had to the development plan, the determination is, unless material considerations indicate otherwise – (a) to be made in accordance with that plan." Section 25(1)(b) relates to national developments. (See Chapter 3 for more details.) Section 37(2) states: "In dealing with such an application the authority shall have regard to the provisions of the development plan, so far as material to the application, and to any other material considerations." This legislation and its interpretation by case law is now examined.

The role of the development plan

In determining a planning application, regard is to be had to the development plan; the determination is, unless material considerations indicate otherwise, to be made in accordance with that plan (1997 Act, s 25(1)(a)). This is known as the "plan-led" system and was introduced by the Town and Country Planning Act 1990, which amended the Town and Country Planning (Scotland) Act 1972, by the introduction of s 18A. This became s 25 of the 1997 Act, now s 25(1)(a) following the 2006 Act reforms. Prior to this, the role of the development plan and material considerations were quite evenly balanced and were regulated by the forerunner of s 37(2) of the 1997 Act: "In dealing with such an application the authority shall have regard to the provisions of the development plan, so far as material to the application, and to any other material considerations." In the Thatcher era of the 1980s, however, the focus of the planning system changed to promoting economic growth (M Tewdwr-Jones (ed), *British Planning Policy in Transition* (1996), p 5). Government policy was that planning permission should be granted unless it would cause "... demonstrable harm to interests of acknowledged importance" (Department of the Environment, Circular 14/85: *Development and Environment*). The decision-maker, therefore, took a wide range of material considerations into account in the decision-making process, the most prominent of which was the encouragement to create employment. During the 1980s, the planning system was also criticised for its "appeal-led" approach. Tewdwr-Jones points out that the statutory development plan documents were not given appropriate weighting in planning decisions and the 1991 Act therefore sought to reverse this trend (M Tewdwr-Jones, "Policy Implications of the 'Plan-Led' Planning System" [1997] *Journal of Planning and Environmental Law* 584).

The plan-led system had been provided for within the legislation for well over a decade when the White Paper *Modernising the Planning System* (2005) was published. Yet, the plan-led system was still regarded as not being fully effective in practice. The White Paper, therefore, stated that the central aim of the modernisation proposals was to reinforce the primacy of development plans. It noted that 70 per cent of local plans had been adopted more than 5 years earlier and that 20 per cent had been adopted more than 15 years earlier (p 12). Out-of-date development plans mean that the plan-led system will not operate effectively. The 2006 Act reforms, therefore, address the process for creating development plans and implementing policies (see Chapter 3). However, the law on the role of the development plan and the implementation of the plan-led system has been developed through case law, and this is considered next.

Judicial interpretation of the role of the development plan

Prior to the introduction of the primacy of the development plan, it was held in *Simpson* v *Edinburgh Corporation* (1960) that the statutory predecessor of s 37(2) required the planning authority to adhere strictly to the development plan. Lord Guest, however, stated that "To have regard to", does not, in my view, mean to slavishly adhere to. It requires the planning authority to consider the development plan, but does not oblige them to follow it" (per Lord Guest at 318). He goes on to explain that the planning authority is to consider all the material considerations, of which the development plan is one (at 319). This judgment is still relevant, as it underlines that the development plan in the UK system is not a blueprint, and even under a plan-led system, it ensures the exercise of discretion. Lord Hope affirmed this position in *City of Edinburgh Council* v *Secretary of State for Scotland* (1997) when he adopted the judgment in *Simpson* to hold that the decision-maker "is at liberty to depart from the development plan if material circumstances indicate otherwise" (at 1114). This endorses the position of the decision-maker to depart from the provisions of the plan, in the light of material considerations. Lord Clyde, in the same case, in delivering the leading judgment confirmed that "the priority given to the development plan is not a mere mechanical preference for it. There remains a valuable element of flexibility. If there are material considerations indicating that it should not be followed, then a decision contrary to its provisions can properly be given" (per Lord Clyde at 1121).

The whole approach of the decision-maker is usefully set out by Lord Clyde in the *City of Edinburgh* case as follows:

> "In the practical application of section 18A (now s 25 of the 1997 Act) it will obviously be necessary for the decision maker to consider the development plan, identify any provisions in it which are relevant to the question before him and make a proper interpretation of them. His decision will be open to challenge if he fails to have regard to a policy in the development plan which is relevant to the application or fails properly

to interpret it. He will also have to consider whether the development proposed in the application before him does or does not accord with the development plan. There may be some points in the plan which support the proposal, but there may be some considerations pointing in the opposite direction. He will require to assess all of these and then decide in the light of the whole plan if the proposal does or does not accord with it. He will also have to identify all the other material considerations which are relevant to the application and to which he should have regard. He will then have to note which of them support the application and which of them do not and he will have to assess the weight to be given to all of these considerations. He will have to decide whether there are considerations of such weight as to indicate that the development plan should not be accorded the priority which the statute has given to it. And having weighed these considerations and determined these matters, he will require to form his opinion on the disposal of the application. If he fails to take account of some material consideration or takes account of some consideration which is irrelevant to the application, his decision will be open to challenge. But the assessment of the considerations can only be challenged on the ground that it is irrational or perverse" (per Lord Clyde at 1122).

It is clear, therefore, that the courts recognise the importance of the development plan, but are still most supportive of the discretionary system. In relation to the exercise of discretion, there are general public law rules and administrative decision-making processes for local authorities, which must be applied to planning decisions. In particular, general principles were articulated by Lord Greene MR in *Associated Provincial Picture Houses Ltd* v *Wednesbury Corporation* (1948) as follows:

"if, in the statute conferring the discretion there is to be found expressly or by implication matters which the authority ... ought to have regard to, then in exercising the discretion it must have regard to those matters. Conversely, if the nature of the subject matter and the general interpretation of the Act make it clear that certain matters would not be germane to the matter in question, the authority must disregard those irrelevant collateral matters" (at 228).

Furthermore, the decision must not be *Wednesbury* unreasonable, that is "a decision no reasonable body could have come to" (per Lord Greene MR at 231). The decision-maker, therefore, if having followed due process, is perfectly entitled to depart from the development plan if material considerations so indicate. *St Albans District Council* v *Secretary of State for the Environment and Allied Breweries Ltd* (1993) was the first High Court decision in England to consider the meaning of the new legal provisions to introduce the plan-led system. The Deputy Judge interpreted it by accepting that, while there was now a legal presumption in favour of the development plan, this presumption was not a strong one. It, therefore, could at least in law, if not in policy, be relatively easily rebutted. This decision set the tone for all future judicial interpretation of the legislative provision implementing the plan-led system.

Scottish Ministers' Guidance: the development plan

Scottish Planning Policy (2010), para 25 states:

> "the Town and Country Planning (Scotland) Act 1997 requires decisions to be made in accordance with the development plan unless material considerations indicate otherwise. Material considerations should be related to the development and use of land ... Where a proposal is in accordance with the development plan, the principle of development should be taken as established and the process of assessment should not be used by the planning authority or key agencies to revisit that."

This policy statement goes further than the judicial interpretation of the plan-led system. It is seeking to fetter discretion by suggesting that the plan should always be followed, notwithstanding the existence of material considerations which might indicate a departure from the plan in certain circumstances. However, this is policy guidance, and not law. Their Lordships in *City of Edinburgh* were clearly alert to the difficult nature of planning decision-making: and Lord Clyde in particular is aiming to impose some rigour in the process of decision-making which encompasses the inherent flexibility of the British planning system in the context of a plan-led system. The flexibility is provided by the concept of "material considerations", considered next.

Material considerations

The term "material considerations" has been integral to the planning system in the United Kingdom since its introduction in 1947. In dealing with an application for planning permission, the decision-maker "shall have regard to the provisions of the development plan, in so far as material to the application and to any other material considerations" (Town and Country Planning (Scotland) Act 1947, s 12(1)). It has been replicated in all succeeding planning Acts (now 1997 Act, s 37(2)). There is no statutory definition of the term and Sir Desmond Heap observes that what constitutes a material consideration has been the subject of dialogue, dissertation, discussion and disagreement in planning and legal circles over the years (Sir Desmond Heap, "R v Westminster City

Council, ex parte Monahan" [1998] *Journal of Planning and Environmental Law* 3). A basic test for a material consideration was established by Cooke J in *Stringer v Minister for Housing and Local Government* (1970): "any consideration which relates to the use and development of land is capable of being a material consideration" (at 1293). A second test was articulated by Lord Keith in *Tesco Stores Ltd v Secretary of State for the Environment* (1995) when he stated (at 764) that material means relevant. These are general tests which merely assist with the scope of a material consideration as the list of matters that could be said to be concerned with the use and development of land or with the character of the use of land is open-ended (*Clyde & Co v Secretary of State for the Environment* (1977)). Much will depend on the circumstances and the proposal on each individual planning application and the relevance of a particular material consideration to a particular planning application.

Examples of material considerations as established by case law

1 Creation of a precedent In *Collis Radio v Secretary of State for the Environment* (1975) it was held that a local planning authority can properly take into account the possibility that to grant planning permission for a development, unobjectionable in itself, might set a precedent and make it difficult for the authority to refuse planning permission for similar development on other sites, thus leading to undesirable proliferation. However, in order to rely on this ground there must be some evidence that this is a realistic possibility (*Poundstretcher v Secretary of State for the Environment* (1989)). A previous decision by the court concerning the same application site is a material consideration in determining a subsequent application, as there is a need for consistency in decision-making (*North Wiltshire District Council v Secretary of State for the Environment* (1992)). Similarly, a previous decision refusing a planning permission is a material consideration in a subsequent application for the same site. A previous decision is potentially relevant not because there was a duty to decide similar cases in the same way, but because it was desirable that there was consistency in decision-making (*R (on the application of Rank) v East Cambridgeshire District Council* (2003)).

2 Protection of private interests Protection of private interest can be a material consideration, notwithstanding that the main object of planning control is to restrict private development for the benefit of public interest. *Stringer v Minister for Housing and Local Government* (1970) recognises, however, that there will be times when the protection of a private interest may become a material consideration which facilitates the public interest.

3 Preservation of existing use The desirability of retaining an existing permitted use is a matter which can validly be taken into account in determining a planning application, provided that the planning authority's reason for seeking the continuation of the existing use is a proper planning one. In *Clyde & Co v Secretary of State for the Environment* (1977), an application to convert part of a building from residential use to office accommodation was refused: it was held that the undesirability of permitting the change, which would intensify an existing housing shortage, was a material consideration. In *Westminster City Council v British Waterways Board* (1985), Lord Bridge expressed that a rather high standard was appropriate for this threshold, that of a balance of probability.

4 An undesirable use A decision-maker may refuse a planning application, where granting it would perpetuate or consolidate an undesirable use and make it less likely that the use would diminish in intensity or be replaced by a less desirable one (*W H Tolley & Son Ltd v Secretary of State for the Environment* (1998)).

5 Financial viability In *Sosmo Trust v Secretary of State for the Environment* (1983), it was held that the lack of financial viability could be material, where a failure to grant permission could result in the building being left empty. *R v Westminster City Council, ex parte Monahan* (1989), however, established that "any other material considerations" could properly include "financial considerations" as long as the decision is based on planning grounds and not some ulterior motive. Financial viability is now regularly regarded as a material consideration (*Samuel Smith Old Brewery (Tadcaster) v Secretary of State for Communities and Local Government* (2008)).

6 The economic and social impact of development In *Council for National Parks Ltd v Pembrokeshire Coast National Park Authority* (2004), the court held that the decision-maker was entitled to take into account the economic benefits of the proposed development in the form of employment opportunities.

7 Environmental control The principal issue in *Gateshead Metropolitan Borough Council v Secretary of State for the Environment* (1994) was the proper approach to be adopted by the Minister where two statutory regimes applied and, to an extent, overlapped. Environmental considerations were recognised as a material consideration, but it was held that the weight to be given to environmental issues and the power to control them under other legislation is a matter for the decision-maker.

8 The cost of the proposed development: not a material consideration   In *J Murphy & Sons Ltd* v *Secretary of State for the Environment* (1973), the Minister, in deciding whether to grant planning permission for local authority development, had refused to take into account the fact that the site would be a particularly expensive one to develop.

9 Fear of harm   The fear of harm which a proposed development would cause to residents has been recognised as a material consideration (*Newport Borough Council* v *Secretary of State for Wales* (1997)). However, fears and concerns about crimes, based on assumptions about future occupants and not supported by evidence, would not be regarded as a valid material consideration (Neil Stanley, "Public Concern: The Decision Maker's Dilemma" [1998] *Journal of Planning and Environmental Law* 919).

10 Planning gain   The law regarding the extent to which planning benefits or gain are permissible, and therefore become material considerations, was clarified by the 1995 *Tesco* case (see p 112). Such benefits are regarded as a material consideration, if connected to the proposed development.

11 Sustainability   The sustainability of a proposed development has been recognised as a material consideration (*Horsham District Council* v *First Secretary of State; Devine Homes plc* (2004)).

12 Personal circumstances of the applicant   In *Westminster Council* v *Great Portland Estates* (1985), it was held that "what is really to be considered is the character of the use of land, not the particular purposes of a particular occupier". However, the personal circumstances of the applicant may be a material consideration, especially where an adverse decision would bring personal hardship on the applicant. In *South Cambridgeshire District Council* v *Secretary of State for Communities and Local Government* (2008), the decision-maker took account of the fact that the disabled child of the applicant needed to remain on a particular site to enable her to obtain ongoing medical care and attend a nearby special school. The court held that the special needs of the disabled child are material considerations justifying the grant of permission contrary to the development plan to enable the family to remain on-site.

These are just some examples, which in the circumstances of a particular planning case have either been identified as material considerations or as not. In each case all relevant material considerations need to be identified and taken into account in the decision-making process. The weight to be attached to a material consideration has also been the subject of judicial comment.

Weight of a material consideration

All relevant material considerations need to be taken into account. The weight to be given to a material consideration, however, is a matter for the decision-maker. This point was clarified in *Tesco Stores Ltd* v *Secretary of State for the Environment* (1995). In this case, the House of Lords held that the Secretary of State had indeed identified and considered the offer by Tesco to contribute to the new ring road as a material consideration. He had, however, given it no weight in the decision-making process. It is "entirely for the decision-maker to attribute to the relevant consideration such weight as he thinks fit" (per Lord Keith at 764). Lord Hoffmann (at 784) takes the concept further by stating that "if the decision to give the consideration no weight is based on rational planning grounds, then the planning authority is entitled to ignore it". The process of identifying material considerations is, therefore, a matter of law. Provided all the relevant material considerations are identified and considered, it is then up to the decision-maker to decide how much weight should be given to the material consideration in the circumstances of the case.

Scottish Ministers' Guidance: material considerations

Scottish Ministers have provided guidance on defining a material consideration in Annex A of Circular 4/2009. It draws on the *City of Edinburgh* case and also provides two main tests in deciding whether a consideration is material and relevant:

- it should serve or be related to the purpose of planning and should therefore relate to the use and development of land; and
- it should fairly and reasonably relate to the particular application.

The guidance states that it is for the decision-maker to decide if a consideration is material and to assess both the weight to be attached to each material consideration and whether individually or together they are sufficient to outweigh the development plan. It also points out that where development plan policies are not directly relevant to the development proposal, material considerations will be of particular importance (Circular 4/2009, Annex A, para 4). It explains that the range of considerations which might be considered material in planning terms is very wide and can only be determined in the context of each case. It also provides examples of possible material considerations, including representations made on a planning application and relevant national policy (Circular 4/2009, Annex A, para 5). It concludes by stating that the planning system operates in the long-term public interest. It does not exist to protect the interest of one person or business against the activities of another. In distinguishing between public and private interest, the basic question is whether the proposal would unacceptably affect the amenity and existing use of land and buildings which ought to be protected in the public interest, not whether owners or occupiers of neighbouring or other properties would experience financial or other loss from a particular development (Circular 4/2009, Annex A, para 6).

COMMENT ON THE DECISION-MAKING PROCESS

The introduction of a plan-led system in the early 1990s did marginally fetter the discretion of planning authorities. In Scotland, s 25 of the 1997 Act has provided a little more certainty for developers. There was no real change in the way decisions were made and the system still allowed flexibility for decision-makers. Nevertheless, it was clear that over the years the time taken to prepare and adopt or approve plans has militated against an effective plan-led system. Ironically, it was the introduction of the plan-led system and the consequent shift of focus to preference for sites in the plan, that concentrated effort at plan approval stage by developers and third parties. From the 1990s onwards, therefore, local plan inquiries became longer and indeed challenges to the plan process meant that some development plans at quite advanced stages of preparation had to be abandoned.

The 2006 Act clearly recognised this and has made real attempts to enhance the system of plan making. Scotland now has a new development planning hierarchy and it is hoped that the new procedures will enable plans to be kept up to date. The post-2006 Act reforms certainly strengthen the Scottish plan-led system and this is endorsed by *Scottish Planning Policy*. Government guidance, however, appears to fetter discretion and the ability to depart from the development plan. Nevertheless, legislation and case law are clear: Scotland has a plan-led discretionary system that provides a focused approach to rationally interpreting the plan, which can accommodate new circumstances and respond appropriately to development proposals. The position regarding national developments, however, has changed. Once they have been identified in the NPF, there appears to be no further opportunity to exercise discretion (see Chapter 3 for more details). Overall, however, the underlying aims of the Scottish planning system have not been overly affected by the legislative reforms. There remains an assumption of a planning regime based on the creation of development plans which guide development through the planning application approval system. This is combined with reasonable administrative discretion provided by the legislation and supported by the courts.

Essential Facts

Making the decision: procedures

- The procedure for checking that a planning application is valid, once submitted, is laid down in the Town and Country Planning (Development Management Procedure) Regulations 2008 and Circular 4/2009: *Development Management Procedures*.
- Neighbour notification, consultations, publicity and entry to the planning register follow validation.
- Pre-determination hearings are provided for major developments where they are significantly contrary to the development plan and for national developments (1997 Act, s 38A). Procedure at the hearing is at the discretion of the planning authority but guidance is provided by Annex F to Circular 4/2009.
- Applications of national interest can be called in for determination by Scottish Ministers (Town and Country Planning (Notification of Applications) (Scotland) Direction 2009).
- The Cairngorms National Park Authority can call in for determination applications within its boundary.
- National and major applications should usually be determined within 4 months of validation.
- Local applications and applications for approval, consent or agreement of the planning authority as a consequence of a condition attached to a grant of permission should usually be determined within 2 months of validation.

Making the decision: law

- The decision–making process is governed by ss 25(1) and 37(2) of the 1997 Act.
- Section 25 introduced a plan–led system, but it is not a blueprint and material considerations can result in a departure from the plan. This provides flexibility and is a hallmark of the British planning system (*City of Edinburgh Council* v *Secretary of State for Scotland* (1997)).
- In exercising discretion and making planning decisions these must not be unreasonable by *Wednesbury* standard.
- Material considerations must (1) relate to the use and development of the land (*Stringer* v *Minister for Housing and Local Government* (1970) and (2) be relevant and not remote from the planning application to which they relate (*Tesco Stores Ltd* v *Secretary of State for the Environment* (1995)).

Essential Cases

Simpson v Edinburgh Corporation (1960): the development plan need not be slavishly adhered to.

Stringer v Minister for Housing and Local Government (1970): establishes tests for material considerations.

City of Edinburgh Council v Secretary of State for Scotland (1997): Lord Clyde provides a practical application of s 25. The decision–maker must:

- consider the development plan;
- identify any relevant provisions and make a proper interpretation of them;
- consider whether the development proposed in the light of the whole plan does or does not accord with it;
- identify all the other material considerations which are relevant to the application;
- note which of them support the application and which of them do not;
- assess the weight to be given to all of these considerations;
- decide whether there are considerations of such weight as to indicate that the development plan should not be accorded priority.

Tesco Stores Ltd v Secretary of State for the Environment (1995): the House of Lords held that the Secretary of State had identified and considered the offer by Tesco, to contribute to the new ring road, as a material consideration, but that he had given it no weight in the decision-making process. It is "... entirely for the decision maker to attribute to the relevant consideration such weight as he thinks fit" and "if the decision to give the consideration no weight is based on rational planning grounds, then the planning authority is entitled to ignore it".

Moray Council v Scottish Ministers (2007): "[The decision-maker's] starting point will be the development plan; considered if need be in the light of national planning guidance. Having regard to the development plan framework and the nature of the proposal, he must decide what are the determining issues. With those issues in mind, he must make his findings in fact on the nature of the proposal and its probable effects. It is for him to decide what lines of evidence are material to the determining issues and what conclusions are to be drawn from them. The [decision-maker] must then decide in the light of his findings how he resolves the determining issues. This involves the exercise of his planning expertise and judgment." (Lord Gill)

8 THE EFFECT OF A PLANNING DECISION

The decision on a planning application can have a number of implications. In many cases it will be the trigger for development to take place. It may, however, merely be the starting point: for example, if the application is only for planning permission in principle. Approval of planning permission enures for the benefit of the land on which the development is permitted and is transferred with the ownership of the land (1997 Act, s 44(1)) (although it is possible in exceptional cases for personal planning permission to be granted). The decision on a planning application, even if it is for approval, does not necessarily mean that development will go ahead. A planning approval for residential development on agricultural land, for example, will raise the value of land. This may be the only purpose of an application and, once approval has been obtained, the site is then sold. This chapter will provide an overview of the effect of a decision on a planning application. It will highlight the changes brought about by the 2006 Act reforms in relation to implementation of planning decisions.

THE DECISION NOTICE

The decision notice is a very important document. As the name suggests, it sets out the decision on a planning application: whether the planning application has been approved or refused. If it has been approved, it lists the conditions and the reasons for attaching them. If it has been refused, the reasons for refusal are set out. It also provides the date of the decision, which is important for review and appeal purposes. The 2006 Act reforms also include some changes to the decision notice: in particular, that reasons for approval must now be indicated on the notice. The Town and Country Planning (Development Management Procedure) (Scotland) Regulations 2008 and Circular 4/2009 set out the detailed requirements for planning decision notices.

The planning authority must provide a decision notice to the applicant or their agent, in relation to applications for planning permission or for approval of matters specified in conditions attached to planning permission in principle (Town and Country Planning (Development Management Procedure) (Scotland) Regulations 2008, reg 28). This should be done within the prescribed time periods for determining the application. The decision notice has certain requirements (1997 Act, s 43(1A)) and must specify the following:

- the development with which it is concerned;
- the date of the decision;
- the reasons for approving the application;
- the reasons for any conditions attached to the permission; or
- the reason for refusing planning permission; and
- the rights of review/appeal.

Interpretation of the decision notice should be given its ordinary and natural meaning (*Wyre Forest District Council* v *Secretary of State for the Environment* (1989)). Permission can be granted for less than the original application, provided that the sense of the application is not substantially altered (*Bernard Wheatcroft Ltd* v *Secretary of State for the Environment* (1982)). Where an environmental statement has been submitted, as part of the EIA process, the notice should state that environmental information has been taken into account by the decision-maker. (See Chapter 6 above for more detail on EIA.)

Planning Circular 4/2009 provides specific information that must be included in the decision notice, including:

- general information about the development upon which the decision was made;
- duration of a planning permission where a planning authority has directed that different time periods apply to those in ss 58 and 59 of the 1997 Act;
- where a s 75 agreement is to be entered into, the decision notice must specify where the terms (or a summary of them) can be inspected (para 4.96); and
- approval of matters specified in conditions attached to a planning permission in principle must, in addition to the minimum set out in para 4.95, include a description of the matter in respect of the approval, consent or agreement that has been granted or refused.

Everyone who made a written representation on a planning application must be informed of the decision on the planning application and be advised where a copy of the decision notice is available for inspection (Town and Country Planning (Development Management Procedure) (Scotland) Regulations 2008, reg 28(b)).

THE DURATION OF PLANNING PERMISSION

All planning permissions are subject to a time limit by which development must be begun. Rowan Robinson explains that this is "to ensure that land is not undeveloped for an indefinite period of time in the hands of speculators whose only intention is to sell the land at some future date at the enhanced value that permission attracts" (J Rowan Robinson, *The Town and Country Planning (Scotland) Act 1997* (Green's Annotated Acts, 2009), p xx). It was recognised as part of the reform process, that the previous 5-year time period did not provide a sufficient impetus to encourage development. The duration of planning permission was, therefore, addressed by the 2006 Act reforms and the time period reduced, from 5 to 3 years (1997 Act, s 58). The planning permission will lapse at the end of that period if development has not commenced. As far as planning permission in principle is concerned, unless development is started within 2 years from the grant of the last approval of matters specified in the conditions attached to the permission in principle, the planning permission expires (1997 Act, s 59). The overall aim of these changes is for more certainty about the implementation of planning permissions. The planning authority, however, may direct that a shorter or longer period than the statutory period may apply (Circular 4/2009, para 4.102). In a change to the previous procedures, the time period is not a separate planning condition; it is now integral to the consent. An applicant, however, may appeal to Scottish Ministers against the 3-year time period or any different period directed by the planning authority, as if it were a condition.

POST-APPLICATION PROCEDURES

A number of new requirements relating to post-application procedures have been introduced under the 2006 Act reforms.

Notification of commencement of work

The planning authority must be informed of the intended date of the start of a new development, following the grant of planning permission. The planning authority should inform the applicant of this requirement at the time of intimating the decision on the application. Failure to undertake the required notification is a breach of a planning control under s 123(1) of the 1997 Act (see Chapter 11 below for more detail). The information to be provided in the notice is set out in reg 37 of the Town and Country Planning (Development Management Procedure) (Scotland) Regulations 2008.

Notification of completion of development

A notice must also be submitted to the planning authority upon completion of a development which has been subject to a planning approval (para 5.7 of Circular 4/2009). Failure to comply is not in itself a breach of planning control, but may be subject to enforcement action (para 5.9).

Certain classes of development require that a sign (or signs) containing particular information is displayed for the duration of the development (Town and Country Planning (Development Management Procedure) (Scotland) Regulations 2008, reg 38). These are national developments, major developments or developments in Sch 3 to the Regulations. The notice must be in the form set out in Sch 7 to the Regulations. Failure to display a notice, however, does not in itself constitute a breach of planning control (Circular 4/2009, para 5.11).

IMPLEMENTATION OF PLANNING PERMISSION

The action that commences development and therefore implements a planning permission has been the subject of much judicial scrutiny. It is often a crucial point, as in most cases, once the planning permission has been implemented, the time limits cease to apply and the planning permission is kept "alive". A planning permission is regarded as implemented from the earliest date on which any material operation comprised in the development begins to be carried out or the time at which the new use is instigated in cases where the permission is for a change of use only (1997 Act, s 27(1)). It is not necessary for the works to have been undertaken with the intention of carrying out the development (*East Dunbartonshire Council* v *Secretary of State for Scotland* (1998)). Operation in breach of planning permission, however, cannot initiate development. The issue is whether the development is permitted by the planning permission read together with its conditions (*Whitely & Sons* v *Secretary of State for Wales* (1992)).

Completion orders

The ability to keep a planning permission alive by carrying out some limited work can prove problematic for a planning authority, particularly if a site is left barely developed, or half-constructed for many years. Planning authorities, therefore, have powers to require that a development be completed. Section 61(2) of the 1997 Act enables the service of a completion notice on the owner and occupier of land, terminating the planning permission if it is not completed by a certain date. The notice will state that the permission will cease to have effect on the date specified in the notice, which must be at least 12 months from the date of the notice. The notice will not take effect until confirmed by Scottish Ministers. There is a right of hearing before a reporter appointed by the Scottish Ministers, which must be claimed within 28 days of the notice. The authority may withdraw the notice at any time before the date specified in it as the date on which the permission will cease to have effect.

Modification and revocation orders

A planning authority has powers to modify or revoke a planning permission "to such an extent as they consider expedient" (1997 Act, s 65(1)). This can be undertaken at any time before completion: for example, before building operations have been completed or the change of use has taken place. Compensation is payable as a consequence of implementing these orders and therefore it is rarely used (1997 Act, s 76). In exercising this function, planning authorities shall have regard to the development plan and to any other material considerations (1997 Act, s 65(2)).

Refusal of planning permission

The majority of planning applications determined in Scotland are approved. Many applications that have difficult issues associated with them which might result in the application being refused are often resolved through negotiation or are dealt with by way of planning conditions. Inevitably, some applications will be refused. Where an authority refuses planning permission, the notice must state clearly and precisely the reasons for that refusal and it must be accompanied by a notice setting out the applicant's rights of review or appeal (Town and Country Planning (Development Management Procedure) (Scotland) Regulations 2008, Sch 6). Where the refusal is as a result of a direction of the Scottish Ministers or a view from a government department, the decision notice must give full details of that direction or view.

Actions following refusal of planning permission

A refusal of planning permission need not necessarily mean that the type of development proposed will never receive planning permission. It does, however, send out a very clear message to the applicant and the route to the refusal should be examined. The following questions could be helpful in determining whether the applicant should persevere with the proposal:

(1) Was it a delegated decision? If no:

(2) Was it a planning committee decision? If yes:

(3) Did the committee in coming to a decision depart from the officer's recommendation?

In most cases it will be worth discussing with the planning officers involved why the application was refused. If it was a delegated refusal, there will probably be little opportunity for negotiation and amendment, as this would have been undertaken as a matter of course as part of the planning application procedure. (See Chapter 7 above for more detail.) For a committee decision, there might have been a clear issue that was identified in the committee debate that could be addressed. In such cases, a re-submission of an amended proposal addressing the reasons for refusal could be considered. In other cases substantial revision or rethinking of the site and its potential might be required.

It is, however, possible to submit an identical application for consideration by the planning authority; but there are limits to this.

Decline to determine applications for planning permission

A planning authority can decline to determine an application for planning permission following a refusal in certain circumstances (1997 Act, s 39). It can refuse to determine an application if, in the 2 years preceding receipt of the application, the Scottish Ministers on appeal or following a call-in of the application had refused a similar application and since the refusal there had been no significant change to the development plan or to any other material considerations. These have been augmented by the 2006 Act reforms (1997 Act, ss 391A–391D) and now, in circumstances where there has been no appeal or call-in, only one repeat application is allowed, in order to enable the applicants to address the issues arising out of the first application, which has been refused. Subsequently, the planning authority has discretion to decline to determine further applications. This avoids repetitious and vexatious applications which could sometimes wear a planning authority down to eventually approving a development, often to the infuriation of the general public.

Opportunities for challenge

There are various opportunities to challenge a decision on a planning application. These are not confined to those of refusal (see Chapter 12 below). Challenging the decision by way of review or appeal is clearly an option following a decision to refuse planning permission.

Purchase of land following refusal of planning permission

Part V of the Town and Country Planning (Scotland) Act 1997 is concerned with measures that can be utilised to require a planning authority to purchase land following a planning decision. This includes purchase notices (1997 Act, ss 88–99) and blight notices (1997 Act, ss 100–108). These instruments are in fact rarely used. The 2006 Act reforms made minimal changes to these aspects of the regime, mainly to ensure conformity with other parts of the legislation.

THE RELATIONSHIP WITH OTHER CONSENTS

The decision on a planning application, particularly if it is approval of planning permission, is usually part of a chain of consents required prior to the commencement of development. Planning permission will often be obtained first, as this establishes the framework for the development. Other matters such as the details for a building warrant application (also obtained from the local authority) or discharge consent (from SEPA) will flow from the nature of the approval of planning permission. The planning application, however, can only deal with the planning merits of a case and should not be used to determine matters that should properly be dealt with under other legislation. Planning permission, for example, should not be refused on the basis of environmental matters which are governed by other legislation, unless it is clear that authorisation under that regime will be refused (*Gateshead Metropolitan Borough Council* v *Secretary of State for the Environment* (1995)).

Essential Facts

- A decision notice sets out the decision on a planning application. It must specify the reasons for approving or refusing the application; the reasons for any conditions attached to the permission; and the rights of review/appeal (1997 Act, s 43(1A)).
- Planning permission lasts for 3 years (1997 Act, s 58) or 2 years for planning permission in principle, following the last approval of matters specified in conditions (1997 Act, s 59).
- Notification of the commencement and completion of work is now required (Town and Country Planning (Development Management Procedure) (Scotland) Regulations 2008, regs 38 and 39).

- Completion orders can require the completion of a development (1997 Act, s 61(2)).
- Planning permission can be modified or revoked by a planning authority, having regard to the development plan and any other material considerations, before completion of the development (1997 Act, s 65).
- A planning authority can refuse to determine a subsequent planning application following a refusal (1997 Act, ss 391A–391D).
- A planning authority may be required to purchase land following a decision on a planning application (1997 Act, ss 88–99 (purchase notices) and 1997 Act, ss 100–108 (blight notices)).

Essential Cases

Wyre Forest District Council v Secretary of State for the Environment (1989): words in planning decision notices should be given their ordinary and natural meaning.

East Dunbartonshire Council v Secretary of State for Scotland (1998): planning permission is regarded as implemented from the earliest date on which any material operation comprised in the development begins to be carried out or the time when a new use is instigated. It is not necessary for the works to have been undertaken in order to initiate development.

Gateshead Metropolitan Borough Council v Secretary of State for the Environment (1995): planning applications can deal only with planning matters. Following the approval of planning permission, other consents are required in order to initiate development.

9 PLANNING CONDITIONS

Planning conditions shape and mould a planning permission. The ability to attach conditions to planning consents enables the decision-maker to extend their control beyond the basic premise of whether a proposal should be approved or refused. A planning condition, therefore, provides added control and flexibility to the decision-making process. A planning authority does not, however, have a duty to use conditions to make an otherwise unacceptable development acceptable. But if an application is acceptable it should consider whether conditions can be imposed to make the development more acceptable (*Mason* v *Secretary of State for the Environment* (1984)). Such conditions will often relate to the details of the development: for example, the materials or landscaping. It can also include conditions suggested by bodies consulted as part of the determination process, including such areas as road safety, archaeological survey and nature conservation.

The majority of planning applications are approved and, of these, most will have at least one planning condition. The role of planning conditions in the Scottish planning system is, therefore, very important. This chapter will explain their legal limits, their uses and the policy guidance in this area of law. It concludes with some general observations on the use of planning conditions.

STATUTORY PROVISIONS

A general power to impose conditions is established by s 37(1)(a) of the 1997 Act, which provides that "(w)here an application is made to a planning authority for planning permission … they may grant planning permission, either unconditionally or subject to such conditions as they think fit". The statute goes on to provide at s 41 that "conditions may be imposed on the grant of planning permission … for regulating the development or use of any land, under the control of the applicant (whether or not it is land in respect of which the application was made) or requiring the carrying out of works on any such land, so far as it appears to the planning authority to be expedient for the purposes of, or in connection with the development authorised by the permission" (1997 Act, s 41(1)(a)). Rowan Robinson *et al* observe that it is not clear whether this section should be construed as amplifying or restricting the scope of the general power conferred on planning authorities by s 37(1), "although the weight of opinion favours the former" (*Scottish Planning Law and Procedure* (2001), para 9.02). Section 41(1)(b) enables permission to be granted subject to a condition requiring the removal of any buildings or works authorised by the permission, or the discontinuance of any use of land, so authorised at the end of a specified period, and the carrying out of any works for the reinstatement of land at the end of that period.

The requirements of the legislation are therefore for a positive obligation that requires something to be done as part of the planning permission. For example: a new building to be faced in granite; details of a landscaping plan to be submitted to the planning authority or opening a new restaurant only between set times, as part of a change of use consent. The wording of the statute, however, still enables a great deal of discretion in the nature and content of a planning condition, attached to a planning permission. In practice, however, both the approach of the courts and government guidance have narrowed the interpretation of the statute.

JUDICIAL INTERPRETATION OF PLANNING CONDITIONS

The leading case on the validity of planning conditions is *Newbury District Council* v *Secretary of State for the Environment* (1981), in which Viscount Dilhorne establishes three tests for a planning condition. These require that conditions must:

(1) be for a planning purpose and not an ulterior one;

(2) fairly and reasonably be related to the development permitted;

(3) not be so unreasonable that no reasonable authority could have imposed them.

A fourth test (based on *Fawcett Properties Ltd* v *Buckingham County Council* (1961)) can be added that a condition must:

(4) be certain (or may be void for uncertainty).

A final test (based on *British Airports Authority* v *Secretary of State for Scotland* (1979)) is that a condition must:

(5) be necessary.

These tests are now examined.

To serve a planning purpose

The first test is that a planning condition must serve a planning purpose, rather than ulterior ends. The scope of a potential planning purpose is wide ranging (*North East Fife District Council* v *Secretary of State for Scotland* (1992)). It should not be an onerous requirement. For example, a restriction on opening hours for a new restaurant located in a residential area could be imposed to protect occupants of nearby housing from noise and disturbance late in the evening. A condition, however, would be invalid if imposed for an ulterior purpose. In *R* v *Hillingdon London Borough Council, ex parte Royco Homes Ltd* (1974), a condition attached to a planning permission for a residential development required a percentage of the dwellings to initially be leased to people on the local authority's housing waiting list. This was held not to be for a planning purpose and, therefore, *ultra vires*. This decision is clearly of its time and must be considered in the light of the housing legislation and housing duties of local authorities in the pre-Thatcher era. The provision of affordable housing is now integral to many housing development planning approvals and is a requirement secured by way of a s 75 agreement/obligation. (See Chapter 10 below for more detail.)

In the first test, therefore, the distinction between planning and ulterior purposes may be difficult to define, but the crucial point is that once the planning purpose of the condition becomes secondary to any other purpose, then the condition is invalid. In the law relating to material considerations, a planning consideration was defined as one which relates to the use and development of land. (See Chapter 7 above for more detail.) This is helpful, but reinforces the point that satisfying the first test is not difficult. It will therefore usually be clear if a planning authority is attempting to use its powers to fulfil a duty or solve a problem, unrelated to its planning powers.

It is important to note that, although planning relates to the use of the land and not to the user (*Westminster Council* v *Great Portland Estates* (1985)), if the purpose of the condition relates to the use of the land, it will be valid, notwithstanding that it limits categories of users. For example, a condition limiting occupation of cottages to agricultural workers was held to be valid, as it was imposed to further the planning policy of protecting the green belt and did not place an unreasonable restriction on the use of the cottages (*Fawcett Properties Ltd* v *Buckingham County Council* (1961)).

Rowan Robinson *et al* point out, however, that in such cases there are usually two planning purposes involved: first, a policy to restrict development, usually to preserve amenity (eg the green belt in *Fawcett*); then, second, there is the purpose behind the limited exceptions to that policy – in the case of *Fawcett*, this is providing for the agricultural needs of the area. "It is the combination of the two which justifies the restriction on certain types of occupant" (*Scottish Planning Law and Procedure*, para 9.14).

Fairly and reasonably relates to the development

The test for a planning condition to fairly and reasonably relate to the planning application of which it forms part was first identified in *Pyx Granite Co* v *Ministry of Housing and Local Government* (1960) but has been consistently endorsed by subsequent case law. It is explained more fully in *British Airports Authority* v *Secretary of State for Scotland* (1979) as follows:

> "[I]t is enough that there should be a recognised and real relationship between the development and the condition and that it can be affirmed that it is one that is fair and reasonable. That is essentially a question not only of fact, but of judgement and therefore I think it necessarily follows that the question is whether within the particular case, there are to be found facts and circumstances from which the court can conclude that this fair and reasonable relationship exists" (per Lord Cameron at 220).

In that case three applications for development at Aberdeen airport were co-joined in their challenge against the imposition of conditions, *inter alia*, restricting operational flying hours. The condition attached to the permission for British Airways Helicopters Ltd was held not to fairly and reasonably relate to the subject of the application, as the application was not in itself related to the flying of helicopters. It was for a building to provide an office for their flight operations headquarters, for their UK operations as a whole and accommodation for ground training of flying personnel.

In *Newbury District Council* v *Secretary of State for the Environment* (1981), a condition requiring demolition of Second World War temporary buildings did not relate to the change of use, for which planning permission was sought. The condition was therefore struck down for failing to fairly and reasonably relate to the proposed development. Furthermore, in *North East Fife District Council* v *Secretary of State for Scotland* (1992), a condition intended to limit residential development, by restricting the extension of a site's utility connections to other developments, was held to be invalid because it did not reasonably relate to the proposed residential development. Alternatively, a condition attached to a planning permission for an extension to a factory was upheld. It consequently restricted noise level, working hours and emissions to the building as a whole (*Penwith District Council* v *Secretary of State for the Environment* (1977)).

To not be unreasonable

The power to impose a planning condition is subject to the public law doctrine of unreasonableness in the *Wednesbury* sense (see Chapter 7 above). This enables the court to interfere with the exercise of executive discretion, where a decision-maker has used power unreasonably in applying a planning condition. There is clear overlap with the other two tests, as a condition may fail the *Wednesbury* test if it bears no relation to a planning purpose or to the development, the subject of the application. There are, however, many instances where the first two tests are met, but a condition is invalid because it is unreasonable.

In *Hall & Co Ltd* v *Shoreham by Sea Urban District Council* (1964), a condition amounting to a requirement that a road be constructed and dedicated for public use was found to be unreasonable because the local authority was transferring an obligation to provide public facilities to the developer. Another example of an unreasonable condition is a positively worded condition relating to land not under the control of the applicant. This is unreasonable because the applicant will have no power to ensure compliance with the condition (*Birnie* v *Banff County Council* (1954)). Conditions can also not be used to alter the scope of a development which is in substance different from the original application (*Walker* v *City of Aberdeen Council* (1998)).

To be certain

A condition must be capable of being understood in order to be implemented. This is important, as planning legislation enables penalties to be imposed on those who do not comply with condition(s) attached to planning permission (see Chapter 11). A planning condition is only void for uncertainty, however, if "it can be given no meaning or no sensible or ascertainable meaning and not merely because it is ambiguous or leads to absurd results" (per Lord Denning in *Fawcett Properties Ltd* v *Buckingham County Council* (1961) (at 678)). A condition which required that occupation of dwellings "shall be limited to persons whose employment or latest employment is or was employment in agriculture as defined by section 119(1) of the Town and Country Planning Act 1947, or in forestry or in an industry mainly dependent upon agriculture and including also the dependent of such persons as aforesaid" was deemed certain enough to be legally valid. This is because it is the duty of the court to give meaning to those words used in the condition (*Hall & Co Ltd* v *Shoreham by Sea Urban District Council* (1964), per Lord Wilmer LJ at 245).

Necessity

In *British Airports Authority* v *Secretary of State for Scotland* (1979) the Court of Session held that an unnecessary condition was invalid. The power to impose planning conditions was, therefore, also subject to an expediency test. This has been criticised by Collar for taking the courts beyond issues of legal validity into an assessment of the planning merits of the case (N Collar, *Planning* (2nd edn, 1999), pp 155–156).

GRAMPIAN CONDITIONS

In *Grampian Regional Council* v *Aberdeen District Council* (1984), Lord Keith of Kinkel observed that the proposals for development were found by a reporter to be generally desirable. The only aspect regarded as disadvantageous was a traffic problem at a nearby junction. This problem was capable of being solved by the closing of part of a road and it was something which had a reasonable prospect of being achieved. He went on to state (at 67): "In the circumstances, it would have been not only unreasonable, but highly inappropriate to grant planning permission subject to the condition that the development was not to proceed unless and until the closure had been brought about."

"*Grampian* conditions", otherwise known as suspensive conditions, therefore enable planning permission to be granted, subject to a condition which prevents the commencement of the development until a stated prerequisite has been met: for example, providing a visibility splay for an exit to a development, which crosses land which is outwith the application site. This enables planning permission to be granted and negotiations on securing the visibility splay to be conducted separately. The planning permission cannot be implemented until the condition is satisfied.

A "*Grampian* condition", however, is a planning condition regulated by statute, as interpreted by case law and, therefore, it still has to satisfy the other tests. The reasonableness test is particularly important with this sort of condition. This is not the same, however, as satisfying a reasonable prospect test. Lord Keith of Kinkel, in *British Railways Board* v *Secretary of State for the Environment* (1994), held that the function of the planning authority was to decide whether the proposed development was desirable in the public interest and the fact that the applicant will have severe difficulty in satisfying the conditions is not a proper planning ground for refusing the grant of consent. There is no legal principle that there must be a reasonable prospect of the action in question being performed within the lifetime of the permission. Grampian conditions are, therefore, an innovative means of enabling planning permission to be granted.

In considering whether to impose conditions upon a grant of planning permission, a decision-maker is therefore bound by the legal requirements of statute and case law. Further guidance is provided by Scottish Ministers and this is considered next.

NATIONAL GUIDANCE

Scottish Ministers' policy on nationally important land use planning matters is contained within *Scottish Planning Policy* (2010). It sets out the core principles and objectives for key parts of the system (SPP (2010), para 2). It specifically refers to planning conditions under the heading of development management (paras 22–30) and states as follows:

"Conditions imposed on the grant of planning permission can enable development proposals to proceed where it would otherwise have been necessary to withhold planning permission. While the power to impose conditions is wide, it must be exercised in a manner which is fair, reasonable and practicable and the conditions imposed must accord with the established tests set out in Circular 4/1998 *The Use of Conditions in Planning Permissions*" (para 26).

Circular 4/1998 states that planning conditions should only be imposed where they are:

- necessary;
- relevant to planning;
- relevant to the development to be permitted;
- enforceable;
- precise; and
- reasonable in all other respects.

It explains that great importance is attached to these criteria being met so that there is an effective basis for the control of regulation of development which does not place unreasonable or unjustified burdens on applicants and their successors in title (Circular 4/1998, para 2). It also states that planning conditions must not be applied slavishly or unthinkingly and that conditions should be used to achieve a specific end and not to cover every eventuality (Circular 4/1998, para 3).

It should be noted that these government tests are more restrictive than the legal tests established by case law. Nevertheless, applying the circular tests will amount to good practice and should be achievable by planning authorities in most circumstances. On appeal to Scottish

Ministers, conditions may be amended or revoked and circular guidance will be applied. Guidance is also provided in the form of model planning conditions (Circular 4/1998, *Model Planning Conditions – Addendum*). Four examples from the circular are provided below:

Examples of Model Conditions: Circular 4/1998: *The Use of Conditions in Planning Permissions* (Model Planning Conditions – Addendum)

"**Hours of use**: The use hereby permitted shall not operate between [*specify hours and days*].

Occupancy: (*Housing related to agricultural and forestry employment*) Occupation of the dwelling shall be limited to a person solely or mainly employed, or last employed in the locality in [*specify*] or to a widow or widower of such a person and to any dependants.

Garages and outbuildings: All garages and outbuildings shall be used solely for domestic purposes incidental to the use of the dwelling house.

Materials: Development shall not begin until samples of materials to be used (on external surfaces of the buildings) or (in construction of hard standings/walls/fences) have been submitted to and approved in writing by the planning authority. Development shall thereafter be carried out using the approved materials or such alternatives as may be agreed in writing with the planning authority."

Any condition attached to a planning permission must be accompanied by a reason for imposing the condition and set out in the decision notice (see Chapter 8 above). A clear and precise reason for a condition must be given (Circular 4/1998, para 3). The circular also provides examples of appropriate and inappropriate reasons for the imposition of conditions and two are reproduced below:

"*Hours of opening*:

Unsatisfactory reason: In the interests of residential amenity.

Satisfactory reason: To protect occupants of nearby housing from noise/disturbance late in the evening.

Materials:

Unsatisfactory reason: In the interests of visual amenity.

Satisfactory reason: To ensure that the extension matches the external appearance of the existing building and thereby maintains the visual quality of the area."

Procedure for applying planning conditions

Most planning authorities operate a system of standard conditions which have been measured against the circular guidance. Circular 4/1998, however, advises that while the use of standard conditions can be important to the efficient operation of the development control process, such conditions should not be applied as a matter of routine (para 3).

A Local Review Body (LRB) will take advice on the imposition of conditions when making a decision on an application before it for review (see Chapter 12 below). Applications which are considered by planning committee will, if supported by a recommendation of approval, be accompanied by a list of conditions. The committee may decide to impose additional conditions, change one or a number of conditions, or remove a condition. It will be given advice about the validity of its actions, in particular in relation to any additional conditions which it proposes to impose.

REVIEW, APPEAL OR CHALLENGE OF A PLANNING CONDITION

A number of options are available relating to review, appeal and challenge after receipt of a planning permission with planning condition(s) that are considered unacceptable. This chapter deals in overview with the effect of these processes, with particular reference to conditions. (See Chapter 12 for more details.)

Statutory challenge of conditions

The effect of invalidity of a planning condition, if challenged under s 239 of the 1997 Act, is that the preceding determination will be quashed. This was pointed out by the Lord President in *British Airports Authority* v *Secretary of State for Scotland* (1979) and reaffirmed in *North East Fife District Council* v *Secretary of State for Scotland* (1992). The Right Honourable Lord Osborne, therefore, concludes that there can be no question of the excision of an invalid condition from permission, leaving the rest of the permission in force. It would, therefore, only be in some other form of proceeding that the issue of possible severance would arise (*Scottish Planning Encyclopaedia* (2001), A4036).

Review and appeal of conditions

An applicant will have a right of review to either an LRB or Scottish Ministers against the grant of planning permission with an unacceptable condition (see Chapter 12). The subsequent decision may reverse or vary any part of the original decision, no matter what aspect is challenged. This may result in loss of permission or imposition of a more onerous condition.

Development without compliance with conditions

Section 42 of the 1997 Act enables an application to be submitted for planning permission to undertake development without compliance with conditions previously attached. This remedy is available even if the planning permission process has commenced. In deciding the application, the authority can only reconsider the conditions, not the principle of the development as a whole; there is therefore no risk of losing the permission.

Retrospective applications for non-compliance with conditions

An application for retrospective planning permission may also be made for development which was carried out without complying with a condition, subject to which permission was granted under s 33(c) of the 1997 Act.

Enforcement

A developer can intentionally or unintentionally fail to implement a planning condition. This might result in the planning authority instituting enforcement action to bring about implementation. The Breach of Condition Notice was introduced specifically to deal with enforcement of conditions (see Chapter 11 below). A breach of condition does not become immune from enforcement action until the expiration of a period of 10 years.

COMMENT ON CONDITIONS

Conditions are an integral part of the planning system in Scotland. Most planning applications are granted with conditions and the majority of these conditions will be implemented. There are two points to note: first, there are relatively few challenges to conditions; second, although there is some enforcement activity by planning authorities on conditions, particularly since the introduction of the Breach of Condition Notice, this is still relatively limited.

It has been suggested that in the imposition and implementation of conditions there is an elaborate game of bluff (P McAuslan, as quoted in Collar, *Planning*, p 148). Collar explains that applicants are willing to accept conditions which may be invalid, or at least may never be enforced, in order to gain planning permission. Equally, the planning authority may doubt the reality of enforcing a particular condition, but impose the condition anyway, in the hope that the developer will accept and implement it (Collar (1999), p 148). The 2006 Act reforms introduced a requirement for notices to be sent at the start and at the end of the development process (see Chapter 8 above). This should enable the checking of the implementation of conditions and reduce the level of "bluff".

Essential Facts

- Conditions can be attached to planning permission (1997 Act, ss 37(1) and 41).
- Tests have been established by case law that planning conditions should:
  - be for a planning purpose;
  - fairly and reasonably relate to the permitted development;
  - not be unreasonable;
  - be certain.
- "*Grampian* conditions" enable planning permission to be granted, subject to a condition which prevents the commencement of the development until a stated prerequisite has been met (*Grampian Regional Council* v *Aberdeen District Council* (1984)).
- Guidance on conditions is provided by Circular 4/1998: *The Use of Conditions in Planning Permissions*. It sets out more restrictive tests than case law. It states that planning conditions should not be applied slavishly or unthinkingly and that conditions should be used to achieve a specific end and not to cover every eventuality. Model planning conditions are also provided.
- Conditions can be challenged as invalid but if successful the whole planning permission is quashed (1997 Act, s 239).
- Conditions can be reviewed to the local review body or appealed to Scottish Ministers. The subsequent decision may reverse or vary any part of the original planning permission.
- A planning application may be submitted for development without compliance with conditions (1997 Act, s 42) or retrospective planning permission may be sought for carrying out the development without conditions (1997 Act, s 33(c)).

- Conditions can be enforced through a Breach of Condition Notice (1997 Act, s 145) or an enforcement notice (1997 Act, s 127). A condition does not become immune from enforcement action for 10 years.

Essential Cases

Newbury District Council v Secretary of State for the Environment (1981): establishes the three tests for a planning condition (serving a planning purpose; fairly and reasonably relating to the application; and not being unreasonable). A condition requiring demolition of temporary buildings did not fairly and reasonably relate to the proposed development.

Fawcett Properties Ltd v Buckingham County Council (1961): a condition limiting occupation of a cottage to agricultural workers furthered the planning policy of protecting the green belt. A planning condition is void for uncertainty only if it can be given no meaning or no sensible or ascertainable meaning.

British Airports Authority v Secretary of State for Scotland (1979): a condition restricting flying hours did not relate to the development proposal for an HQ building and accommodation for ground training. Directing the direction of take-off and landing of aircraft was also unacceptable. The planning permission for three separate developments at Aberdeen Airport was therefore quashed because of the conditions.

North East Fife District Council v Secretary of State for Scotland (1992): a condition intended to limit residential development by restricting the extension of a site's utility connections to other developments was invalid as it did not reasonably relate to the proposed development.

Hall & Co Ltd v Shoreham by Sea Urban District Council (1964): a condition amounting to a requirement that a road be constructed and dedicated for public use was found to be unreasonable because the local authority was transferring its obligation to provide facilities to the developer.

Grampian Regional Council v Aberdeen District Council (1984): planning permission was granted for a development as there was a reasonable prospect that a road would be closed and thus solve the only issue of concern about the planning application. This case created "*Grampian* conditions" or suspensive conditions.

British Railways Board v Secretary of State for the Environment (1994): this case removed the "reasonable prospect" test for a "*Grampian* condition".

10 PLANNING AGREEMENTS/OBLIGATIONS

Planning agreements and the law and policy related to them have been subject to debate for many years. Indeed it was a topic that was anticipated as ripe for reform even before the 2006 Act, mainly because of the controversies surrounding the concept of planning gain. Although it is a well-known principle that planning consent cannot be bought and sold (Lloyd LJ in *City of Bradford Metropolitan Council* v *Secretary of State for the Environment* (1987)), planning gain, or the provision of benefits for the community in which a development is to be located, is less clear. This practice of planning gain is not unique to Scottish or indeed British town planning. It occurs in most systems, particularly where there is a strong private sector pressure to develop which appears to be held back by regulatory controls. The use of planning agreements in Scotland has increased in recent years, although the actual numbers are still relatively low (in 2006/07 the total number of agreed planning agreements was 396 out of 49,949 planning applications), although the increase in the use of agreements for major housing developments was especially significant (Scottish Government Social Research, *An Assessment of the Value of Planning Agreements in Scotland* (2008)). Political interest in the use of agreements often lies in their ability to secure affordable housing and achieve sustainability. Planning agreements, however, can be used for many purposes and can be created under s 75 of the 1997 Act, as well as s 69 of the Local Government (Scotland) Act 1973 and s 48 of the Roads (Scotland) Act 1984. This chapter deals with only s 75 of the 1997 Act. It covers the existing law and the proposed changes, as well as good neighbour agreements.

At the time of writing, the changes to s 75, to be effected by s 23 of the Planning etc (Scotland) Act 2006, have yet to be implemented (s 23 of the 2006 Act will substitute ss 75, 75A, 75B and 75C in place of the existing s 75 of the 1997 Act). A consultation on the draft regulations was launched in May 2010 and it is anticipated that they will be in place by late 2010. Policy advice, however, has recently been provided by Scottish Government, Planning Circular 1/10: *Planning Agreements*, which points out that the general policy and approach will remain as set out in Circular 1/10 (para 7). Furthermore, Scottish Ministers announced in August 2008 that a planned review of developer contributions was to be postponed and to date no further review has been instigated. In England, however, a

Community Infrastructure Levy, introduced by the Planning Act 2008, was implemented from 6 April 2010 (Pt 2 of the 2008 Act). This levy will operate alongside the planning obligation regime (s 106 of the Town and Country Planning Act 1990, as amended by s 12 of the Planning and Compensation Act 1991). (See R Duxbury, *Telling & Duxbury's Planning Law and Procedure* (14th edn, 2009), Chap 13, for an explanation of the system in England and Wales.)

WHAT IS AN AGREEMENT?

A s 75 agreement is an agreement entered into by the planning authority with any person interested in land in their district for the purpose of restricting or regulating the development or use of land, either permanently or as prescribed by the agreement (s 75(1) of the 1997 Act). It may contain such incidental and consequential provisions (including financial ones) as appear to the planning authority to be necessary or expedient for the purposes of the agreement (s 75(2)). A s 75 agreement can:

- contain provisions which are unconditional or subject to conditions;
- impose a restriction either indefinitely or for a specified period or periods;
- require the payment of a specified sum of money or a sum of money to be ascertained by a formula set out in the agreement, together with the method of payment.

A planning agreement is a contract and is enforceable as such against the person entering into the agreement. If the planning agreement under s 75 is recorded or registered in the Register of Sasines or the Land Register for Scotland, the agreement will be enforceable against singular successors. This feature extends the reach of the planning authority to enter into contracts in pursuance of their functions, which are otherwise enforceable against only the original parties to the agreement. While a planning authority has powers to enter into agreements under other legislative provisions, their use is only to secure direct up-front financial contributions, and, therefore, they are of limited value in matters of planning control. The use of s 75 agreements, if recorded or registered, will provide enforceable restrictions or regulations relating to, for example, occupancy of a house after sale of the property. It also ensures that sufficient finance is set aside to enable operators to meet their restoration obligations, with financial guarantees secured through a s 75 agreement, for example, in connection with renewable energy projects.

THE USE OF SECTION 75 AGREEMENTS

Section 75 agreements provide greater scope for planning requirements than planning conditions (*McIntosh* v *Aberdeenshire Council* (1999)). Policy advice, however, requires that planning authorities should first consider whether a restriction or regulation can be achieved by the use of a planning condition rather than a s 75 agreement (Circular 1/2010, para 13). Agreements should be used only where the obligation cannot be secured by condition or by other means (*Scottish Planning Policy* (2010), para 27). Section 75 agreements, however, can be particularly useful where they can be used to overcome obstacles to the grant of planning permission. The 2008 report, however, commented that "planning agreements are no longer used just to mitigate the impact of development and planning authorities are using agreements to secure contributions towards essential infrastructure (*An Assessment of the Value of Planning Agreements in Scotland*, para 2.6). The provision of public infrastructure is therefore increasingly being provided by the private sector and this is recognised in England and Wales with the introduction of the Community Infrastructure Levy. Although s 75 agreements are, therefore, most often associated with provision of infrastructure, there are many other uses. In *R* v *Plymouth City Council, ex parte Plymouth and South Devon Co-operative Society* (1994), the package of benefits offered in conjunction with an application for a supermarket extended to include: an £800,000 contribution towards a park-and-ride scheme; a £1 million contribution towards the allocation of alternative industrial land; provision of an on-site tourist information centre; a bird-watching hide; and an on-site static art display. A 1992 report also highlighted the diverse and imaginative uses for a planning agreement (Scottish Office, Environment Department, "The Use of Section 50 Agreements" (1992)). These included phasing of developments, reinstatement of land and landscaping after long-term uses, such as mining, agricultural and other occupancy conditions, as well as the provision of bonds. Section 75 agreements, however, can be used only within their legal limits and this is considered next.

THE LEGAL LIMITS FOR PLANNING AGREEMENTS

The law in this area was clarified by a House of Lords decision in *Tesco Stores Ltd* v *Secretary of State for the Environment* (1995). In recent years, however, decisions in the English courts have widened the scope and validity of planning obligations, while new policy guidance in Scotland imposes strict tests on the use of planning agreements (Circular 1/2010:

Planning Agreements). The balance between law and policy in Scotland is now set out.

The Court of Appeal in *Good* v *Epping Forest District Council* (1994) (in addressing s 52 of the Town and Country Planning Act 1971, broadly equivalent to s 75 of the 1997 Act) held that the test for validity of a planning agreement was twofold:

(1) it had to serve a planning purpose; and

(2) it must not be "unreasonable" in the *Wednesbury* sense.

If the s 75 agreement was to be regarded as a material consideration, to be taken into account in the determination of the planning application, there was a third test:

(3) there must be a link or relationship between the planning agreement and the planning application.

Each test is now considered.

Planning purpose

The purpose of the planning agreement, as set down by s 75 of the 1997 Act, is "to restrict or regulate the development or use of land". This has been given a wide interpretation by the courts. For example, in *McIntosh* v *Aberdeenshire Council* (1999), Lord Maclean held that an agreement requiring a developer to construct an estate road which would in part serve his development but also, in part, provide access to facilitate the continuous and progressive development of neighbouring land was *intra vires*. The purpose of the agreement was the restriction of the developer's use of the land, with the aim of ensuring that, should development take place on the neighbouring land, there would be access across the developer's land. This was regarded as a proper planning purpose and appropriate for a planning agreement.

Reasonableness

In *Good* v *Epping Forest District Council* (1994), it was held that the planning authority must act reasonably in the *Wednesbury* sense. This is the second element of the *Good* test of validity for a planning agreement. It is a concept that is well understood in planning law (see Chapter 7 for more details). If, however, parties enter into an agreement which is unreasonable – in other words, there is consent to unreasonableness – there may be an opportunity for challenge. However, Lord Maclean, in *McIntosh* v *Aberdeenshire Council* (1999), held that once a planning agreement had been implemented and acted upon, the developer had waived any challenge to the *vires* of the planning agreement.

Link with the planning agreement

A s 75 agreement is, therefore, valid if it satisfies the two tests above. There is no requirement for a connection between the provisions in a planning agreement and the development for which planning permission is sought. In *Newbury District Council v Secretary of State for the Environment* (1981), Gibson LJ held that the second test laid down for validity of planning conditions to the effect that the conditions must be "fairly and reasonably related" to the permitted development did not apply to planning agreements. The House of Lords then drew a distinction between the validity of the planning obligation and whether such an obligation fell to be regarded as a material consideration in the determination of a planning application. Furthermore, if the s 75 agreement is to be regarded as a material consideration, to be taken into account in the determination of the planning application, it must pass another test. *Tesco* established that there must be a link or relationship with the planning application. Tesco challenged the decision of the Secretary of State, principally on the ground that he had failed to take account of a material consideration, ie an offer to fund a new road. The House of Lords held that the relationship between the supermarket and the new road was material, but at the margins. Lord Hoffmann, in particular, rejected the requirement for a "fairly and reasonably related" test and distinguished the earlier Court of Appeal case of *Plymouth*. *Tesco* therefore clarified that the question of what is a material consideration, is a matter of law (see Chapter 7 for more details). The weight to be attached to a material consideration, however, is a question of fact, for the decision-maker to determine in the exercise of his planning judgement. The House of Lords held that the Secretary of State in this case had had regard to the consideration, but had determined to give it little weight because of the tenuous relationship to the development. Lord Keith of Kinkel clarified the nature of the link between an obligation in a planning agreement and the related planning application. He stated: "[a]n offered planning obligation which has nothing to do with the proposed development, apart from the fact that it is offered by the developer, will plainly not be a material consideration and could be regarded only as an attempt to buy planning permission. If it has some connection with the proposed development which is not *de minimis,* then regard must be had to it." But, the extent, if any, to which it should affect the decision is a matter entirely within the discretion of the decision-maker. The *Tesco* case therefore established the enduring legal tests for a valid agreement and, as these are not arduous, enables much to be included as part of a valid planning gain package.

Community benefits

A range of benefits is often voluntarily provided by developers to communities, particularly in the vicinity of renewable energy developments. This can include community trust funds. It would seem that such a fund could satisfy the validity tests of serving a planning purpose and not being unreasonable. Whether the execution of a planning agreement with a valid community benefit provision is material to the decision to grant planning permission is a separate question for determination. Indeed, *Scottish Planning Policy* (2010) states, however, that such benefits should not be treated as a material consideration unless they meet the tests set out in Circular 1/2010: *Planning Agreements*. The circular is considered next.

PLANNING CIRCULAR 1/10: *PLANNING AGREEMENTS*

Circular 1/10: *Planning Agreements* was published in February 2010. Paragraph 3 states that "the process of negotiating and concluding planning agreements should not slow down the planning process, delaying the benefits of appropriately planned development and adding costs for developers, infrastructure providers and the wider public sector". They should also not be used to obtain a benefit which is unrelated to the nature or scale of the proposed development. The circular sets out five policy tests, advising that planning agreements should only be sought in circumstances where all the following tests are satisfied:

(1) necessary to make the proposed development acceptable in planning terms;

(2) serve a planning purpose and, where it is possible to identify infrastructure provision requirements in advance, should be relevant to development plans;

(3) relate to the proposed development either as a direct consequence of the development or arising from the cumulative impact of development in the area;

(4) fairly and reasonably relate in kind to the proposed development; and

(5) be reasonable in all other respects.

This is a tightening of the policy tests for s 75 agreements as previously set out under Circular 12/1996. It is also a much stricter test than that required by the case law. The Circular, read as whole, places s 75 agreements as a part of the wider planning process in Scotland, one in which the use of agreements will be used primarily to provide infrastructure requirements in a cohesive and measured process linked to the National Planning Framework and the new style development plans.

PLANNING AUTHORITY APPROACH TO SECTION 75 AGREEMENTS

Development plans

Planning authorities have increasingly used development plans to indicate infrastructure and other requirements associated with development, particularly affordable housing. This approach has been reinforced by the 2006 Act reforms and *Scottish Planning Policy* (2010), which states that planning authorities should use the development plan and supplementary guidance to set out their approach to planning agreements (para 27). Planning agreements, according to Scottish Ministers, should be plan-led, thus linking with the 2006 Act reforms and the strengthening of the plan-led system. The benefit to this is that it provides a systematic mechanism for public participation as part of the plan preparation process. Once in the plan, this approach also enables a developer to anticipate the financial implications of proposed developments. It is important, therefore, that plans are kept up to date in order that the s 75 agreement policies in development plans remain relevant. It may be that supplementary guidance will be used to ensure that this is the case (see Chapter 4 for more details). It is expected that the new tranche of development plans in Scotland, introduced under the 2006 Act reforms, will set out clear requirements for developer contributions.

Planning gain officer

Many local authorities have a planning gain officer who negotiates s 75 agreements on behalf of the Council, resulting in some cases in both imaginative and pragmatic additions to developments (S Robertson, "Innovations in Developer Contributions", *Scottish Planner* (January 2006), p 10).

Planning register

The details of s 75 agreements are now placed on the planning register (see Chapter 7 for more details). This was highlighted in the White Paper

Modernising the Planning System (2005) as a way of making the process more transparent (p 32).

PLANNING OBLIGATIONS

Section 23 of the 2006 Act will, when implemented, substitute a new s 75 in the 1997 Act and add new ss 75A–75C. Planning agreements in Scotland will thereafter be renamed "planning obligations". The new legislation will enable unilateral obligations to be made. It will therefore no longer be necessary for the party to be the owner of the land at the time of entering into the obligation. The scope of the obligation is also clarified; in particular, specific reference is made to the payment of "a specified amount" and "periodical sums" (s 75(2) and (3) of the 1997 Act, inserted by s 23(3) of the 2006 Act). A future date can be set at which the obligation will come into effect; or the obligation may be triggered by a specific event – for example, to take effect once a certain stage of a development has been completed. Furthermore, if there is a breach in any requirement of a planning obligation, the planning authority, under the new system, will have default powers. It will be able to carry out the required operations and recover the cost from the person against whom the obligation is enforceable, provided 21 days' notice has been given. These changes will introduce improvements to the operation of the s 75 system in Scotland, which have been advocated for many years and are in line with the regime operated in England and Wales since 1990. In May 2010, the Scottish Government Directorate for the Built Environment issued a consultation on Planning Obligations, including draft regulations. The consultation also covers Good Neighbour Agreements and these are considered next.

GOOD NEIGHBOUR AGREEMENTS

Good neighbour agreements were introduced in the White Paper *Modernising the Planning System* (2005). They had not been part of the consultation prior to the publication of the White Paper and many concerns about their use and appropriateness for the Scottish system were expressed (Scottish Government, *Modernising the Planning System: Analysis of Responses* (2005)). This may be why they are one of the last elements of the 2006 Act reforms to be introduced. There are, however, examples of such agreements in Scotland, negotiated outside the planning system. Friends of the Earth Scotland were instrumental in encouraging their use, supported by their own research (Friends of the Earth Scotland,

"Love thy Neighbour? The Potential for Good Neighbour Agreements in Scotland" (2004)). Good neighbour agreements have been used in other jurisdictions, including the United States of America and New Zealand, and are often associated with righting environmental injustices. For example, landfill sites or quarrying, even when carried out legitimately (ie with the necessary planning permission), can still have a negative impact on the areas in which they are located, by way of noise, dust and increased traffic. Rowan Robinson points out that the objective of a good neighbour agreement is to reconcile economic development with community welfare (*The Town and Country Planning (Scotland) Act 1997*, Green's Annotated Acts (2009), p xxii).

The White Paper explains their use as follows:

> "We recognise the value of local people being able to enter into arrangements with site operators for significant developments which would guarantee them a role in monitoring the way development is carried out. Parties to such an agreement may include the developer of the site, the future operator and a body that is representative of the local community, for example, a residents group or community council ... issues to be covered include hours of operation, patterns and frequency of vehicle movements and the provision of more general information on environmental performance" (p 41).

Section 24 of the 2006 Act, when implemented, will therefore introduce ss 75D–75G of the 1997 Act, to establish good neighbour agreements within the planning system in Scotland. The provisions are similar to the new ones for planning obligations and will provide a legislative framework for voluntary agreements between a developer or landlord and a local community body, such as a community council. An example is provided that an agreement might require a developer to provide information to the community council on the progress of the development and compliance with conditions. Good neighbour agreements are not intended to be used to secure the provision of infrastructure or community benefits and the legislation specifically precludes the use of such agreements to secure financial payments (Government Directorate for the Built Environment, *Consultation on Planning Obligations and Good Neighbour Agreements* (2010), p 8). The consultation also includes draft regulations. It is expected that the provisions for planning obligations and good neighbour agreements will be implemented later in 2010. The Scottish Government intends to publish further guidance on good neighbour agreements when the relevant provisions of the 2006 Act come into force.

Essential Facts

Planning agreements

- Section 75 provides for an agreement between a planning authority and a landowner.
- It restricts or regulates the use of the land and can contain financial and other provisions.
- A s 75 agreement can be registered in the Land Register or the Register of Sasines.
- Planning agreements can be used for a wide variety of purposes: removing obstacles to a planning permission; securing affordable housing; providing infrastructure; controlling occupation of a development; ensuring phasing of a development; providing for long-term after-care and to reinstate and landscape.
- It is often referred to as "planning gain", particularly when community benefits are provided.
- A planning agreement must serve a "planning purpose" and not be unreasonable (*Good* v *Epping Forest District Council* (1994)).
- For a planning agreement to be regarded as a material consideration there must be a link or a relationship between the planning agreement and the planning application (*Tesco Stores Ltd* v *Secretary of State for the Environment* (1995)).
- Guidance is provided in Circular 1/10: *Planning Agreements.*
- Infrastructure and other requirements associated with planning permission and which would be secured by way of a planning agreement are often included in development plans. This will continue under the new system of plans, including the use of supplementary guidance.
- Planning obligations enable the creation of unilateral obligations, clarify the scope of obligations including financial ones and introduce default powers once implemented by new ss 75A–75C of the 1997 Act.

Good neighbour agreements

- Good neighbour agreements, once implemented, will provide a legislative framework for voluntary agreements between a developer or landlord and a local community body (ss 75D–75G).

- The aim is to reconcile economic development with community welfare and will cover issues such as operating hours and intrusive development.
- They will not be used to provide community benefits, infrastructure or financial payments.

Essential Cases

Good v Epping Forest District Council (1994): established that planning agreements should serve a planning purpose and not be unreasonable.

R v Plymouth City Council, ex parte Plymouth and South Devon Co-operative Society (1994): the Court of Appeal established that a planning agreement had to be fairly and reasonably linked to the planning application in order to be a material consideration and to be taken into account in the decision-making process. The planning gain package for a new supermarket included a £1 million contribution to alternative industrial land, £800,000 towards a park-and-ride scheme, a tourist information centre and a bird-watching hide.

Tesco Stores Ltd v Secretary of State for the Environment (1995): the House of Lords held that the offer to fund a link road around Witney in Oxfordshire did have a link with the planning application for an out-of-town shopping centre, as there was an existing traffic problem and the supermarket would exacerbate it. It was regarded as being material, although at the margins (Lord Hoffmann). An offered planning application which had nothing to do with the proposed development, apart from the fact that it was offered by the developer, would plainly not be a material consideration and could be regarded as an attempt to "buy" planning permission (Lord Keith).

11 ENFORCEMENT

The effectiveness of the planning regime in Scotland is that it has an enforcement regime as its backstop because "[t]here is not much point in having a sophisticated system for controlling development, unless there are effective provisions for enforcing control" (J Rowan Robinson *et al*, *Scottish Planning Law and Procedure* (2001), para 12.01). This chapter provides an overview of the planning enforcement system in Scotland. The regime has been changed by the 2006 Act reforms, but less so than in other areas of planning law. (For a detailed explanation of the enforcement framework, see Rowan Robinson *et al*, *Scottish Planning Law and Procedure*, Chap 12.)

BACKGROUND TO PLANNING ENFORCEMENT REFORM

Enforcement has been described as "the poor relation in what some would consider an already impoverished service" (G U'ren, "Planning Enforcement Charters" (2007) 121 *SPEL* 57). To some extent this was addressed by reforms which came into effect in 1992, through the Planning and Compensation Act 1991, with the relevant provisions subsequently incorporated into the 1997 Act. These followed a critical report of the enforcement system throughout the UK by Robert Carnworth QC (Department of the Environment, *Enforcing Planning Control* (1989)). The operation and the effect of the changes of the revised system in Scotland were reviewed in 1997 (Scottish Office, *Review of Planning Enforcement* (1997)). This report recognised that, although the changes had been beneficial, there was still much room for improvement, particularly by making better use of existing powers, rather than the introduction of new ones. New planning guidance was issued at that time. The mechanisms and processes of enforcement, however, were still regarded as poor and were, therefore, revisited as part of the most recent planning reform agenda.

The Scottish Executive White Paper *Modernising the Planning System* (2005) noted that, for many, their first contact with planning was through the enforcement regime and "the system may seem to be lengthy and 'unfair' in that there appears to be no penalty for unauthorised development". It concluded that the basic principles of the current framework did not need to be changed, but that there was scope for radically improving the delivery of planning enforcement. It identified strengthening the enforcement regime, as a major contribution towards making the planning system fairer and more balanced (*Modernising the Planning System*, p 42). As U'ren pointed out, "[i]t had become the talisman for restoring much needed public trust in the whole (planning) system" ("Planning Enforcement Charters" (2007) 121 *SPEL* 57).

Some new and extended powers have therefore been introduced by the 2006 Act. Nevertheless, Rowan Robinson comments that, although the new measures should help to strengthen the regime, "it is doubtful if they are likely to lead to a radical improvement in the system" (*The Town and Country Planning (Scotland) Act 1997*, Green's Annotated Acts (2009), p xxii). Scottish Ministers were of the view that a culture change was required in the operation of the enforcement system, rather than just legislative reform; and, to that end, from 1 April 2007, all planning authorities are required to prepare an Enforcement Charter (1997 Act, s 158A). This is a statement of the planning authority's policies on taking enforcement action and an explanation as to how members of the public are to bring any alleged breach of planning control to the attention of the authority. Following preparation, Enforcement Charters are to be published, kept under review and lodged with Scottish Ministers. Scottish Government guidance on this topic was published in 2009: *Planning Enforcement Charter – A guide to enforcing planning controls*.

Enforcement is dealt with in Pt VI of the 1997 Act, as amended by the 2006 Act, which introduces:

- notification of initiation and completion of development (1997 Act, ss 27A–27C) (see Chapter 8 above for more details);
- notices requiring submission of retrospective planning applications (1997 Act, s 33A);
- fixed penalty notices (1997 Act, ss 136A and 145A);
- temporary stop notices (1997 Act, ss 144A–144D).

Planning Circular 10/2009: *Enforcement*, including Annexes A–L, also provides detailed guidance on the approach to enforcement, as well as guidance on the law. It makes some important changes to the previous guidance and also provides advice on the new elements of the enforcement regime, introduced under the 2006 Act reforms.

This chapter deals with the following topics:

- what is a breach of planning control?;
- planning contravention notices (PCNs);

- taking enforcement action;
- stop notices;
- temporary stop notices;
- interdict;
- fixed penalty notices;
- time limits on enforcement action;
- certificates of lawful use or development.

WHAT IS A BREACH OF PLANNING CONTROL?

A breach of planning control can take a number of forms. It is defined by s 123 of the 1997 Act as follows:

- carrying out any development without the required planning permission; or
- failing to comply with any condition or limitation subject to which planning permission has been granted; or
- instituting or carrying out development without the required notification procedures.

A breach of planning control can therefore be the undertaking of unauthorised building, engineering, mining or other operations. It can be a material change of use which required planning permission, but has proceeded without it (1997 Act, s 123(1)(a)). Failure to comply with a condition or limitation subject to which planning permission has been granted can also be a breach of planning control (1997 Act, s 123(1)(b)). Two new seemingly small, but potentially very powerful, monitoring tools have also been introduced by the 2006 Act reforms, which also constitute a breach of planning control: initiating development without displaying a notice in accordance with s 27A(1) of the 1997 Act; and carrying out development without displaying a notice in accordance with s 27C(1) of the 1997 Act.

Breach of planning control is not normally a criminal offence; however, once enforcement proceedings have begun, non-compliance can lead to a criminal prosecution. The 2006 Act reforms, however, introduced fixed penalty notices, in particular to deal with developers who consistently breach planning control. It is important to base a decision on whether to take enforcement action on appropriate information; one mechanism for obtaining information is the Planning Contravention Notice and this is dealt with next.

PLANNING CONTRAVENTION NOTICE (PCN)

The planning contravention notice (PCN), introduced by the Planning and Compensation Act 1991, was designed to fill a particular information gap in the system. A PCN may be served wherever it appears to the planning authority that there may have been a breach of planning control in respect of any land (1997 Act, s 125(1)). The PCN may be served on anyone who is the owner or occupier of the land in question (1997 Act, s 125(1)(a)) or on a person who is using or carrying out operations on the land (1997 Act, s 125(1)(b)). The planning authority may, therefore, serve several notices on different people in respect of the same suspected breach (Circular 10/2009, Annex D, para 3). There is no need for the authority to obtain clear evidence of a breach of control before issuing a PCN. It is sufficient for the authority to suspect that a breach may have occurred (Circular 10/2009, Annex D, para 4). The recipients of the notice are required to provide the information requested in the notice (1997 Act, s 125(2) and (3)). At the planning authority's discretion, the notice may allow recipients an opportunity to make a response to the matters it raises, and to make representations at a specified time and place (1997 Act, s 125(4)). Circular 10/2009 advises that planning authorities should offer this opportunity where they consider that it may assist resolution of an alleged breach (Annex D, para 8). Serving a PCN does not constitute "taking enforcement action" for the purposes of s 123 of the 1997 Act. It is, however, an offence not to comply with any requirement in the notice. The PCN procedure is less draconian than that of the enforcement notice, but it is nevertheless intrusive and compliance is mandatory if properly served (*R v Teignbridge District Council, ex parte Teignmouth Quay Co Ltd* (1995)). The contents of the response to the PCN will assist the planning authority in deciding whether enforcement action should be taken. The mere service of the notice, however, may result in an operation or use being stopped or altered. A retrospective planning application may also be submitted.

TAKING ENFORCEMENT ACTION

It is important to understand that there is no legislative requirement for a planning authority to react to a breach in its area, by taking enforcement proceedings. This is a decision to be made by the planning authority exercising its powers of discretion. It is not obliged to issue an enforcement notice, even if it is satisfied that a breach of consent has occurred, unless the refusal to take action is arbitrary or capricious (*Perry* v *Stanborough* (*Developments*) (1977)). The planning authority, however, appears to be obliged at least to consider whether action is required (*R* v *Stroud District Council, ex parte Goodenough, Usborne and Tomlin* (1982)). Advice on the general approach to enforcement has been provided by Scottish Ministers in Circular 10/2009: *Planning Enforcement*, para 7, as follows:

> "Planning authorities have a general discretion to take enforcement action against any breach of planning control if they consider such action to be expedient, having regard to the provisions of the development plan and any other material considerations. When they are considering whether any particular formal enforcement action is an expedient remedy for unauthorised development, planning authorities should be guided by the following considerations:
>
> • Planning authorities, under the provisions of the 1997 Act, have primary responsibility for taking whatever enforcement action may be necessary in the public interest, in their administrative area.
>
> • Decisions in such cases, and any resulting action, should be taken without undue delay. Failure to do so could constitute grounds for a finding of maladministration by the Scottish Public Services Ombudsman.
>
> • In considering any enforcement action, the planning authority, with regard to the Development Plan, should consider whether the breach of control would affect unacceptably either public amenity or the use of land and buildings meriting protection in the public interest.
>
> • Enforcement action should always be commensurate with the breach of planning control to which it relates. For example, it is usually inappropriate to take formal enforcement action against a trivial or technical breach of planning control which has no material adverse planning implications … However, planning authorities should be aware that failure to take enforcement action against a breach of planning control could be subject to a referral to the Scottish Public Services Ombudsman."

However, the Circular goes on to stress that:

> "The integrity of the development management process depends upon the planning authority's readiness to take effective enforcement action when necessary. Public respect for the development management system is undermined if unauthorised development, which is unacceptable on its planning merits, is allowed to proceed without any apparent attempt by the planning authority to intervene before serious harm to amenity results from the breach" (para 9).

A failure to take enforcement action may also amount to a failure to protect the human rights of a neighbour (European Convention on Human Rights, Art 8).

Taking enforcement action is defined as issuing:

*   an enforcement notice (1997 Act, s 127);
*   a breach of condition notice (1997 Act, s 145);
*   a notice requiring a retrospective application for planning permission (1997 Act, s 33A).

Enforcement notices

Planning authorities may at their discretion issue an enforcement notice where it appears to them that there has been a breach of planning control and that it is expedient to do so, having regard to the development plan and to any other material considerations (1997 Act, s 127(1)). Copies of the notice must be served on the owner and the occupier of the land to which it relates and any other person with an interest in the land, if the authority considers that interest to be materially affected by the notice (1997 Act, s 127(2)(b)). The notice must be served within 28 days of its issue and not less than 28 days before the date on which it is due to take effect (1997 Act, s 127(3)). Enforcement notices require landowners and developers who have breached planning control to correct the breach and the notice sets out the action or work that is required to make the development acceptable in planning terms. The content of the notice is therefore very important: the requirements are set out in s 128 of the 1997 Act; and are also dealt with in Circular 10/2009, Annex G. Section 129 deals with variation and withdrawal of enforcement notices. Details of the enforcement notice will be recorded in the planning register (Town and Country Planning (Enforcement of Control) (No 2) (Scotland) Regulations 1992 (as amended).

An enforcement notice can be appealed at any time before the notice takes effect (1997 Act, ss 130–134). The White Paper, *Modernising the Planning System* (2005), stated that the procedure for appeal against an enforcement notice would be re-examined. Appeal rights have been retained, following the 2006 Act reforms, but an enforcement notice appeal no longer constitutes a deemed application for planning permission. Guidance on appeals is provided by Circular 9/2009, Annex G, paras 21–22.

It is an offence to be in breach of an enforcement notice (1997 Act, s 136) and the planning authority can take action either through the issue of a fixed penalty notice or by seeking prosecution (Circular 9/2009, Annex G, para 38).

Breach of condition notices

The breach of condition notice was introduced specifically to target breaches of planning conditions (1997 Act, s 145). It was considered that the enforcement notice was too cumbersome a procedure and that a quicker and simpler enforcement tool was required. It has been most successful in enforcing planning conditions and is regularly utilised by planning authorities. A breach of condition notice may be used as an alternative to or in conjunction with an enforcement notice. It may be served on any person who is carrying out or has carried out the development or any person having control over the land. It must specify the steps to be taken or the activities which must cease and it allows a period of time, which is not less than 28 days, for compliance. The period of time may be extended by a subsequent notice by the planning authority. There is no right of appeal to Scottish Ministers; however, the recipients may make representations to the planning authority, if they believe the notice is unreasonable. The planning authority may withdraw the notice at any time and this does not affect the planning authority's power to serve a further notice.

It is an offence to be in breach of a breach of condition notice. A notice is breached if at any time after the expiry of the compliance period any condition specified in the notice has not been complied with and the specified steps have not been taken or the specified activities have not ceased. The planning authority may either issue a fixed penalty notice or prosecute (Circular 9/2009, paras 20 and 21).

Retrospective application for planning permission

The creation of a notice that enables a planning authority to require an application for planning permission for development which is in breach of planning control is inserted into the 1997 Act as s 33A. This is formalisation of normal local authority good practice, which previously encouraged the submission of a planning application, in order to regularise unauthorised development. The intention in introducing this notice is to encourage the submission of a retrospective planning application, which would then allow the planning authority to consider the grant of planning permission, subject to any conditions or limitations that would make the development acceptable in planning terms (Circular 10/2009, Annex C, para 3). The issue of the notice requiring the retrospective planning application constitutes taking enforcement action. Section 33(4) of the 1997 Act provides that the power to grant retrospective planning permission is not to apply if, before the date of the application, an enforcement notice has been issued in respect of the development. Fees for retrospective planning permission are set at a higher rate than other applications, in order to deter unlawful development. The details of the notice are set out in Circular 10/2009, Annex C.

STOP NOTICES

A stop notice may be served by a planning authority if it is considered "expedient" that an activity ceases quickly (1997 Act, s 140). An enforcement notice must also have been served, but an enforcement notice does not take effect for at least 28 days. It must be issued, however, before the enforcement notice to which it relates takes effect. The stop notice must specify the "relevant activity" which is required to cease and which is the reason for serving the notice (1997 Act, s 140(2)). It must specify the date on which it is to take effect, which must be in at least 3 days and not more than 28 days after the date when the notice is served (1997 Act, s 140(7)). There are some exceptions to the service of a stop notice (1997 Act, s 140(3)–(6)). A site notice must be displayed to publicise the fact that a notice has been served (1997 Act, s 141).

The intended effect of serving a stop notice will usually be to halt the breach of control or the specified activity. There is no right of appeal against a stop notice and it is an offence to contravene or cause to contravene it (1997 Act, s 144). A stop notice ceases to have effect if the related enforcement notice is withdrawn and in a number of other circumstances (1997 Act, s 141). The service of a stop notice may result in the requirement to pay compensation (1997 Act, s 143(1)–(4)). This, combined with the quick decisions that are required to be made in relation to issuing a stop notice, means they are used only with great caution by planning authorities.

TEMPORARY STOP NOTICES

The 2006 Act reforms allow a planning authority to issue a temporary stop notice which takes effect immediately it is issued (1997 Act, ss 144A–144D). Unlike a stop notice, it does not require the issue of an enforcement notice. Its effect, however, is the same and requires the immediate cessation of an activity from the moment it is displayed on a site. It can be followed in due course by other enforcement action. Rowan Robinson describes it as "a breathing space [for planning authorities] while they decide how best to respond" (Rowan Robinson, *The Town and Country Planning (Scotland) Act 1997*, p xxiii). There are exceptions to the use of a temporary stop notice; there is no right of appeal against it and there is an entitlement to compensation in certain circumstances. The detail about their use is provided in the Town and Country Planning (Temporary Stop Notice) (Scotland) Regulations 2009 and guidance is provided in Annex I to Circular 10/2009.

INTERDICT

The civil law remedy of interdict can be used if either a breach of planning control has occurred or there is evidence that one is likely to occur (1997 Act, s 146). The planning authority may apply either to the sheriff court or to the Court of Session and it is at the discretion of the court as to whether it is granted. In *Perth and Kinross Council* v *Lowther* (1996) it was held that an interdict could be employed more widely than an enforcement notice. *The Review of Planning Enforcement* (Scottish Office, 1997) found that interdict, when used, has proved to be very effective. However, in practice, it is rarely employed by local authorities.

FIXED PENALTY NOTICES

Fixed penalty notices offer an alternative to criminal prosecution as the offender is given an opportunity to pay a monetary penalty. The 2006 Act reforms introduced s 136A to the 1997 Act, which enables a planning authority to issue fixed penalty notices for non-compliance with an enforcement notice, and s 145A of the 1997 Act for non-compliance with a breach of condition notice. The payments received are then retained by the planning authority. The level of fixed penalty has been prescribed in the Town and Country Planning (Amount of Fixed Penalty) (Scotland) Regulations 2009. The rationale behind the introduction of a fixed penalty notice is that it is quicker, cheaper and easier than preparing a prosecution and therefore the planning authority is more likely to utilise this mechanism. Furthermore, the longer the developer fails to rectify the breach, the higher the potential penalty.

TIME LIMITS ON ENFORCEMENT ACTION

The legislation imposes a time limit on the taking of enforcement action. There are different time limits for different types of development. Section 124(1) of the 1997 Act requires that enforcement action can be taken only within 4 years of the date on which the operations were substantially completed. "Operations" extends to building, engineering, mining and other operations, in, on, over or under the land. If the breach of planning control extends to any building for use as a single dwelling house, s 124(2) provides that enforcement action may be taken only within 4 years of the breach. This time limit applies to both where the change of use is development without planning permission and where it involves a failure to comply with a condition or limitation of a planning permission. Guidance on the meaning of "substantially completed" and "use as a single dwelling house" is provided in Annex A of Circular 10/2009.

There is a limitation on taking enforcement action after 10 years in cases of a material change of use of land, except change of use to a single dwelling house, where no planning permission has been obtained or the development is in breach of a condition or limitation to which planning permission is subject (1997 Act, s 124(3)). These time limits apply to the first taking of enforcement action; however, there are circumstances where supplementary enforcement action can be taken outwith the normal time limits (s 124(4)(a) and (b)). General guidance on time limits is provided in Annex A of Circular 10/2009.

CERTIFICATE OF LAWFUL USE OR DEVELOPMENT

A mechanism is provided by ss 150–153 of the 1997 Act for establishing the planning status of land and whether an existing or proposed development is considered lawful for planning purposes. If it is established, the local authority provides certification of the lawful use or development. This is useful either to ensure that an activity does not result in enforcement action or to counter the possibility of enforcement action, for example by the issue of a planning contravention notice. (See Chapter 5 for more details.)

Essential Facts

- A breach of planning control is carrying out development without the required planning permission; failure to comply with a condition or instituting development without the required notification procedures (1997 Act, s 123).
- A planning contravention notice can be served whenever it appears to the planning authority that there has been a breach of planning control. The recipient is to provide the information in the notice. It is an offence not to comply with the notice (1997 Act, s 125). The information provided can assist the planning authority in deciding whether to take enforcement action.

- Enforcement action will be taken by a planning authority only where there is a breach of planning control and it is expedient to do so, having regard to the development plan and to any other material considerations.

- Taking enforcement action is issuing:
  - an enforcement notice (1997 Act, s 127);
  - a breach of condition notice (1997 Act, s 145);
  - a notice requiring a retrospective application for planning permission (1997 Act, s 33A).

- An enforcement notice requires the breach to be corrected and should set out the measures to be taken and the date it is to take effect (1997 Act, s 128). It can be appealed (1997 Act, ss 130–134). It is an offence to be in breach of an enforcement notice (1997 Act, s 136).

- Breach of condition notices target non-compliance with planning conditions. It must specify the steps to be taken or the activities which must cease in order to comply with a condition. There is no right of appeal and it is an offence to breach the notice (1997 Act, s 145).

- A retrospective planning application requires the submission of a planning application in order that the planning authority can consider granting planning permission subject to conditions (1997 Act, s 33A). Fees for retrospective planning applications are set higher than usual in order to deter unlawful development.

- Stop notices are served if a planning authority considers it expedient that an activity cease quickly (1997 Act, s 140). An enforcement notice must also have been served. It is an offence to contravene a stop notice. There is no appeal. Compensation may be payable.

- Temporary stop notices take effect immediately (1997 Act, ss 144A–144D). A new form of remedy, they provide some "breathing space" for planning authorities. Compensation may be payable.

- Interdict can be used if there is a breach of planning control or there is evidence that one is likely to occur (1997 Act, s 146).

- Time limits for enforcement action are 4 years from the date when "operations" were substantially completed (1997 Act, s 124(1)) and 10 years for a material change of use (1997 Act, s 124(3)).

- Guidance is provided by Circular 10/2009: *Enforcement*.

12 REVIEW AND APPEAL

The appeal system is the "sharp end" of the planning process. In the year ending 31 March 2009, the Directorate for Planning and Environmental Appeals (DPEA), processed 1,412 appeal cases. This is less than 3 per cent of all planning application decisions in Scotland. The 2006 Act reforms, effective in this area from 3 August 2009, created an entirely new system of handling planning appeals. However, the reform of the appeal process, like other aspects of the planning reform agenda, has been protracted (Scottish Executive, Consultation paper, *Modernising Public Inquiries* (June 2003) and Scottish Executive, Consultation paper, *Rights of Appeal in Planning* (April 2004)). Much of the consultation process was centred on the question as to whether the right of third party appeal should be introduced in Scotland. This issue dominated not only the debate about the appeal system, but also the reform of the Scottish planning system as a whole, notwithstanding that it was not eventually included in the 2005 White Paper. Arguably much of the detail and the implications of the new appeal system, as proposed in the White Paper, and then published in the Bill, was not widely appreciated at that time. One aspect of reform, the proposed Local Review Bodies (LRB), however, "caused considerable controversy during consultations over the Bill as the planning authority are made judges in their own cause" (J Rowan Robinson, *The Town and Country Planning (Scotland) Act 1997* (Green's Annotated Acts, 2009), p xvi). The LRB will now deal with many of the appeals which would previously have been considered by the DPEA. This chapter, therefore, considers local review bodies, appeal to Scottish Ministers and, in brief, further legal challenge. It concludes with reference to mediation within the planning system. The new regime is implemented by amendments to the 1997 Act, plus the Town and Country Planning (Schemes of Delegation and Local Review Procedure) (Scotland) Regulations 2008; Circular 7/2009: *Schemes of Delegation and Local Reviews*; Town and Country Planning (Appeals) (Scotland) Regulations 2008; and Circular 6/2009: *Planning Appeals*.

LOCAL REVIEW BODIES

The new system of development management introduced the planning hierarchy, which distinguishes three levels of development: national, major and local. Local developments will largely be decided without recourse to a planning committee, by an "appointed person" under delegated powers (1997 Act, s 43A(1)–(7)). Where a person so appointed (a) refuses an application for planning permission; (b) grants it subject to conditions; or (c) has not determined it within 2 months, the applicant may require the planning authority to review the case. The rationale behind this type of review was set out in the White Paper as follows: "[a] key benefit would be that the vast majority of all appeals would hence forth be decided quickly and decided locally, recognising that local authorities are best placed to take decisions on local matters" (p 25). Rowan Robionson observes that a distinction has been made between the decision of the planning officer which is not subject to review and which is treated as that of the planning authority on the one hand, and the decision of the planning officer which is subject to review and which is not to be treated as the decision of the authority, but a decision of the planning officer (*The Town and Country Planning (Scotland) Act, 1997*, p xvii). Nevertheless, concerns have been consistently raised that this new process would not comply with Art 6 of the European Convention on Human Rights (ECHR): everyone is entitled to a fair and public hearing within a reasonable time by an independent and impartial tribunal. The Scottish Government argued that there was no Convention rights issue, if the overall context of decision-making in Scotland is considered. Poustie, however, concluded that the overt lack of independence is problematic (M Poustie, "Planning Reforms in Scotland" [2007], *Journal of Planning and Environmental Law* 489 at 517). At the time of writing, no ECHR challenge arising from the decision of a Local Review Body has been made. A planning authority, however, may decide to determine an application, which would otherwise be determined by the appointed officer, as a delegated decision. In such cases, an application would instead be considered by way of a planning committee (s 43A(6)). Such a decision route retains the right of appeal to Scottish Ministers (1997 Act, s 47).

Local Review Body: procedure

An applicant may require the planning authority to review a planning application dealt with through delegated powers according to s 43A(8) of the 1997 Act when:

- the application is refused;
- it is approved subject to conditions;
- it is not determined within 2 months (or 4 months on Sch 2 EIA cases).

This is undertaken by the Local Review Body and the detailed procedures are set out in the Town and Country Planning (Schemes of Delegation and Local Review Procedure) (Scotland) Regulations 2008 and Planning Circular 7/2009: *Schemes of Delegation and Local Reviews.*

Regulation 9 requires the applicant to give notice in writing within 3 months of the date of the decision or the failure of the planning officer to determine the application. The notice must be provided on a form obtained from the planning authority and must include all the information set out in reg 9(3). Importantly, reg 9(4)(a) requires that all matters which the applicant intends to raise in the review must be set out in or accompany the notice of review. Furthermore, all documents, materials and evidence which the applicant intends to rely on in the review must accompany the notice of review (reg 9(4)(b)). This front loading of the process is new to the Scottish planning appeal system and now characterises appeals at all levels, not just the Local Review Body. (An exception to this, however, may be possible in relation to submission of material at a later stage to Local Review Bodies under reg 15 and the Hearing Session Rules.)

The Local Review Body consists of at least three elected councillors (membership and role of the LRB is explained at paras 28–30 of Circular 7/2009). The LRB has 2 months in which to determine the review. On receipt of the notice of review, the LRB must within 14 days acknowledge the notice of review and give notice of the review to each interested party. Any interested party may, within 14 days from the date of the notice, make representations in respect of the review to the LRB and the LRB then needs to send a copy of any representations received from third parties to the applicant and give the applicant a further 14 days in which to make comments on those additional representations. The LRB has a number of routes to final determination of the review, but it should be noted that, at this stage in the process, more than half of the decision-making time of 2 months will already have elapsed.

Determination: Local Review Body

The LRB can make a decision on the review based on the existing information: reg 12 of the Schemes of Delegation and Local Review Procedure Regulations 2008 enables the LRB to consider that it has sufficient information to enable it to determine the review without further procedure. If it decides it does not have enough information or representations, the LRB can hold a pre-determination meeting to consider the manner in which the review (or any stages of the review) is to be conducted (reg 14). It must give notice of the holding of such a meeting and of the date, time and place where it is to be held.

The review can be conducted by written submissions, a hearing session or a combination of the two (reg 13(2)). All these routes will also include a site visit (reg 13(3) and (4)). If the review is to proceed by written submissions, the LRB can request such further representations or information from the applicant or any other body. This must also be circulated to other parties who have 14 days to respond.

Hearing session: Local Review Body

The LRB may decide that a determination will involve a hearing session and can appoint an assessor to advise it on such matters that it specifies. Written notice of the hearing must be given to the applicant and other interested parties. The LRB should also set out in writing the matters that are intended to be considered and only those matters should be considered at the session (Circular 7/2009, para 43). All parties must respond within 14 days, confirming whether they intend to appear at the hearing session (Sch 1 to the Regulations). Parties then provide a hearing statement and any copies of documents to which they intend to refer in advance of the hearing. It is for the LRB to determine the procedure at a hearing session (para 45). Paragraph 47 of Planning Circular 7/2009 states that the regulations are clear, that the hearing process should take the form of a discussion, led by the LRB and that cross-examination should not be permitted unless the LRB considers it necessary to ensure a thorough examination of the issues.

Decision: Local Review Body

Once all the information and representations have been received and the oral hearing completed (if required), the LRB will undertake a site inspection (reg 16). The LRB will then make a determination on the review of the planning application. The LRB must issue a written decision following its review and the matters to be covered are set out in s 43A(12)(a) of the 1997 Act and reg 21. In particular, this must include details of the provisions of the development plan and any other material considerations to which the LRB had regard in determining the application.

If the review is against a failure of the "appointed person" (planning officer) to determine the application and the LRB subsequently fails to review the application within 2 months, an applicant can appeal to Scottish Ministers under s 43A(17) of the 1997 Act. Otherwise, there is no further appeal to Scottish Ministers. An application, however, can be made to the Court of Session within 6 weeks of the date of the decision under s 239 of the 1997 Act.

The introduction of this new local review procedure for delegated decisions made by a person appointed under the terms of s 43A of the 1997 Act and described above will reduce the actual number of appeals to Scottish Ministers. This is considered next.

APPEALS

The planning system introduced in the post-war period provided for all appeals against refusal or failure to take decisions on planning applications to be made to central government. In Scotland, appeal was to the Secretary of State for Scotland, until devolution in 1999, when appeal was to Scottish Ministers. The legislative reforms effective from 3 August 2009, however, created an entirely new system for the handling of planning appeals. Appeals to Scottish Ministers are generally only available for national and major developments. In most cases, a reporter is appointed (the "appointed person") from the DPEA to determine the appeal on behalf of Scottish Ministers. This is known as a delegated appeal. On the occasions when Scottish Ministers choose to determine the appeal themselves, the "appointed person" reports to Scottish Ministers to enable them to reach a decision on the appeal. This aspect of the process remains the same; however, the role of the reporter and the DPEA has changed. The new rules on appeal procedure apply equally to appeals determined by Scottish Ministers, as to those decided by reporters. The legislative provision for appeals to Scottish Ministers is found in ss 47, 47A and 48 of the 1997 Act, augmented by the Town and Country Planning (Appeals) (Scotland) Regulations 2008, as amended by the Town and Country Planning (Miscellaneous Amendments) (Scotland) Regulations 2009 and Planning Circular 6/2009: *Planning Appeals*.

Appeals: procedure

The first major change to the appeal procedure is the reduction in time available to take an appeal. The period in which an applicant can lodge an appeal is reduced from 6 months, under the old regime, to 3 months under the 2006 Act reforms. The notice of appeal needs to be served within a period of 3 months from the date of the decision notice, or, in the case of an appeal against non-determination of a planning application, 3 months from the expiry of the prescribed period for determining the application (Town and Country Planning (Appeals) (Scotland) Regulations 2008, reg 3(2)). Once the prescribed period has passed there is no scope for an appeal to be lodged. The justification for this change was to reduce uncertainty for objectors and planning authorities (*Modernising the Planning System* (2005), p 32).

An appeal to Scottish Ministers is generally only available for major and national developments. There are five routes to appeal:

(1) against a decision of the planning authority to refuse planning permission (for a major or a national development);

(2) against a condition or conditions attached to the grant of planning permission by a planning authority on a major or national development;

(3) failure to determine a planning application for a major or national development within the statutory period;

(4) failure by an LRB to review an application within 2 months which had previously failed to be determined by an "appointed person"; and

(5) against a decision of a planning authority on an application, which would normally be determined by the appointed officer, but in the case in question was considered by way of a planning committee.

Appeals: process

An appeal to Scottish Ministers must be made on the prescribed form and contain the prescribed information (Town and Country Planning (Appeals) (Scotland) Regulations 2008, reg 3) and it will not be accepted if it does not contain this information (Circular 6/2009, para 9). All matters that the appellant intends to raise at the appeal must be set out in the notice of appeal and all documents and any other evidence that the appellant intends to use to support the case should accompany the appeal. An appellant must also include a note of what matters the appellant considers should be taken into account in determining the appeal and by what procedure the appellant wishes the appeal to be conducted (Town and Country Planning (Appeals) (Scotland) Regulations 2008, reg 3).

Section 32A of the 1997 Act restricts the variation of applications once they have gone to appeal. Under s 47A, parties will not be able to raise any new matter during the appeal that was not before the planning authority at the time it took the decision, unless it can be demonstrated that it could not have been raised at the time, or there have been exceptional circumstances. Poustie explains that appeals will no longer be *de novo* hearings of applications (Poustie [2007] *Journal of Planning and Environmental Law* 489 at 507). It is considered that it will be easier for third parties to engage in the appeal process, if less new material is introduced at a later stage. Circular 6/2009 reiterates that s 32A provides clarity about the extent to which the appeal process should focus on the proposal that was considered by the planning authority. In particular, para 12 states that where an applicant considers that it would be beneficial to revise a proposal, a new planning application should be submitted for consideration by the planning authority.

The appellant must notify the appeal to the planning authority and this process is regulated by reg 4 of the Town and Country Planning (Appeals) (Scotland) Regulations 2008. The planning authority has 21 days to respond, using a form provided by DPEA, with specified documents and information. The appellant then has 14 days to respond further, if any new matters are raised by the planning authority. Paragraph 17 of Circular 6/2009 explains that representations previously lodged with the planning authority by interested parties will be taken into account before a decision is reached on appeal; there is, therefore, no need or expectation for the same matters to be raised again. Nevertheless, under reg 5, third parties and statutory consultees are notified of the appeal by the planning authority and have 14 days to make representations. The planning authority then has 14 days to respond to third parties. This completes the exchange of information process for appeals. The next stage is the procedure for determination.

Determination: appeals

The reporter may at this stage consider that there is sufficient information to determine the appeal. Regulation 7 of the Town and Country Planning (Appeals) (Scotland) Regulations 2008 enables the decision to be made, without there being any further procedure or information gathering. Paragraph 21 of Circular 6/2009 makes it clear that as soon as the reporter considers that sufficient information has been provided to enable a decision to be made, the regulations allow the determination of the appeal.

If further procedures are considered necessary, it is the reporter who decides the nature of these procedures. The preferences of the parties must be taken into account, but there is no requirement for formal notice of the choice of procedure to be provided, nor for reasons to be given for the choice. It is entirely within the discretion of the reporter, and it therefore does not follow that, where either the appellant or the planning authority has requested a public local inquiry, an inquiry would be arranged (Circular 6/2009, para 21). The reporter can obtain further information and additional representations in order to determine the appeal, by one or a combination of procedures set out in reg 8. These are: further written submissions, hearing sessions, inquiry sessions or a site inspection. The reporter will identify each of the matters on which further information is needed and also the procedure to be used to obtain it. This will be clearly set out in a procedure notice (Circular 6/2009, para 22). The reporter, however, may at any stage in the appeal process decide that it is necessary to carry out a site inspection before making a decision. Site visits can be accompanied or unaccompanied and procedures are set out in reg 11 of the Town and Country Planning (Appeals) (Scotland) Regulations 2008. There are also provisions relating to pre-examination meetings, although Circular 6/2009 indicates that it is likely that these will only be required in a small number of complex cases. Where appropriate the reporter will use a pre-examination meeting to consider with the appellant, the planning authority and third parties how the appeal or a particular aspect of it can best be conducted efficiently or expeditiously.

Written submissions

The majority of planning appeals in the past were dealt with by way of written submissions. Notwithstanding the changes in the appeal regime, this will still be an important route for determination. Regulation 10 of the Town and Country Planning (Appeals) (Scotland) Regulations 2008 sets out the procedure for seeking further written submissions on the appeal. The appointed person is free to seek additional representations or information from the appellant, the planning authority or from any other body or person and details of the procedure will be provided in the procedure notice. This information should be sent to all parties specified in the procedure notice, including the appellant and the planning authority, and all parties then have an opportunity to send comments on such further information to the reporter within 14 days, with copies being sent to all relevant parties. Circular 6/2009 advises that the timetables for the provision of information must be observed and late submissions may not be taken into account in the final decision on the appeal.

Hearing sessions

A hearing session is intended to take the form of a discussion led by the reporter and formal cross-examination will not be allowed. Schedule 1 to the Town and Country Planning (Appeals) (Scotland) Regulations 2008 sets out the hearing session rules. These provide the reporter with scope to determine what procedure or range of procedures should be followed at a particular hearing. The specified matters to be considered by way of a hearing are to be set out by the reporter in a procedure notice. The rules provide discretion for the procedure the reporter thinks appropriate to follow during the hearing. Circular 6/2009 advises that they also provide a framework to ensure that the relevant parties have clear notice of the hearing session, the other participants in the process and clarity about issues and evidence to be considered at the hearing session (para 28). Those entitled to appear at a hearing session may be required to send a hearing statement and any supporting documents to the other parties entitled to appear at the hearing and to the reporter (Sch 1, rule 4). At the start of the hearing session, the appointed person is to explain the procedure that they intend to adopt, taking account of submissions made by any of the parties entitled to appear. Parties may be represented or, where two or more persons have a similar interest, one or more may appear for the benefit of some or all (para 29).

Inquiry sessions

The rules for inquiries are set out in Sch 2 to the Town and Country Planning (Appeals) (Scotland) Regulations 2008. The inquiry will only deal with the matters upon which the reporter considers further information is required, as set out in the procedure notice. The reporter has the responsibility for publicising the inquiry, but may also require the planning authority to undertake additional publicity. The appellant, the planning authority and only third parties who made representations, or third parties whom the reporter wishes to make representations into specified matters, are entitled to appear at the inquiry. They will receive a written notice from the reporter about their requirement to appear at the inquiry and they must confirm their intention to attend the session within 14 days of the date of the notice. Those appearing at the inquiry are usually required to provide an inquiry statement. This should set out the particulars of the case relating to specified matters, provide a list of documents to be relied upon and a list of other persons who are to speak at the inquiry session, including the matters to be covered by each person and their relevant qualifications. This must be circulated to the appellant and the planning authority. Both the appellant and the planning authority will provide precognitions (statements), but these should not exceed 2,000 words in length.

At the start of the inquiry the reporter is to state the procedure for conducting the session. The rules require the reporter to explain the order in which specified matters are to be considered and the order in which those entitled to appear are to be heard. Parties may be represented or, where two or more persons have a similar interest, one or more may appear for the benefit of some or all. Those entitled to appear at an inquiry session may call evidence, cross-examine witnesses and make closing statements. The reporter can refuse to permit this wherever it is considered to be irrelevant or repetitious. New evidence can be taken into account following the conclusion of the examination procedure; however, the reporter must give the appellant, the planning authority and other relevant parties an opportunity to make representations on the evidence before a decision can be made on the appeal.

Decision: appeals

An appeal can be allowed or dismissed (1997 Act, s 48(1)(a)) or any part of a decision by a planning authority may be reversed or varied (whether the appeal relates to this part or not) (s 48(1)(b)). The decision made either by a reporter or Scottish Ministers is in the form of a reasoned decision letter. The appellant, the planning authority and third parties must be notified that a decision has been made and informed of where a copy of the decision notice is available for inspection.

Expenses

Expenses do not follow success and the parties involved in a planning appeal are normally expected to meet their own costs (N Collar, *Planning* 2nd edn (1999), pp 242). Collar explains that appropriate grounds for claiming expenses are: unreasonable behaviour which has caused the party applying for the award of expenses to incur unnecessary expenses, either because it should not have been necessary for the case to go to appeal, or because of the manner in which the party against whom the claim is made has conducted proceedings (N Collar, *Planning* (2nd edn, 1999), pp 242–243). In the year to the end of March 2009, there were 131 claims for expenses on appeals, with a 27 per cent success rate (DPEA: Review 2008–2009). The new system of dealing with appeals will probably result in a reduction in applications for expenses.

Comment on the appeal process

The new system ushers in a less inquisitorial process for appeals to Scottish Ministers on planning matters. The changes are controversial, although at the time of writing their impact has really yet to be known and it is appropriate merely to highlight the main changes and make some comment. The overarching change, reflected in the new Local Review Body, as well as the appeals system, is the front loading of the process. Unless there are exceptional circumstances, all the information is to be provided at the start of appeal. Rowan Robinson points out that, notwithstanding that development management is an iterative process, "[t]his presumably reflects in part the very limited opportunity to consult with the public and other interested parties over any such new matter during an appeal" (*The

Town and Country Planning (Scotland) Act 1997 (2009), p xix). A second and notable change is the reduction in the time limit to take an appeal; again, this also applies to LRBs. The reduction in the period for appeal was regarded as controversial, both at the White Paper and passage of the Bill stage, not least because a similar reform introduced in England and Wales was quickly abandoned. Third, it is now the reporter who determines the procedure for the appeal, and a range of mechanisms can be used in any one case. Again, this is also the case for LRBs. The parties to an appeal can only indicate their preferred procedure and the reporter will have the final say on the procedure or range of procedures. Interestingly, an examination of the first 6 months of the new system concludes that there appears to have been a steep drop in the number of appeals for which there is any oral (inquiry or hearing) process (R Seaton, "Getting Heard at Appeal: The First Six Months of the New Appeal System" (2010) 138 *SPEL* 39). Circular 6/2009 claims that the changes to the appeal process "are intended to ensure that examination procedures are proportionate and efficient; that the appeal process is transparent and fair; and that the decisions are both robust and based upon a review of the proposals that were originally considered by the planning authority". Only time and experience will reveal whether the revised processes will deliver these objectives, although an early reaction is that "there is a debate to be had about whether the current handling of appeals tends more towards speed" (Seaton, p 41). Only time and experience will reveal whether the revised process will deliver these objectives, although on early reaction is that "… there is a debate to be had about whether the current handling of appeals tend more towards speed".

FURTHER CHALLENGE

The Town and Country Planning (Scotland) Act 1997 provides a number of opportunities for further challenge of a planning decision. In relation to appeals, there is a 6-week period in which to take a statutory review challenge to the Court of Session (1997 Act, s 239). This considers the manner in which a decision was made rather than the merits of the case. This is a rarely utilised route (only nine challenges in 2008–09 and ten in 2007–08: DPEA Review 2008–2009). Nevertheless, statutory challenge is an important control mechanism, particularly in relation to process. The outcome of a successful challenge, however, might be that the Court of Session refers the case back to the decision-maker, who may be able to reach the same decision, but in a legal manner: and, therefore, as Collar comments, a pyrrhic victory (Collar, *Planning*, p 245).

Judicial review is a means by which the administrative decisions of public bodies, including planning authorities and Scottish Ministers, can be challenged on the basis of illegality, procedural impropriety or irrationality. A petitioner, however, must have standing or title to sue, as well as "sufficient interest", to do so. This severely limits those who can engage in this process. The Report of the Scottish Civil Courts Review (2009) includes some recommendations which, if implemented, could have far-reaching implications for the role of judicial review in the planning system. These include the introduction of a single test of "sufficient interest to sue" and protective costs orders. Such changes would widen access to the courts in planning cases. Other measures are proposed by the Review that would speed up the process.

The existence of the judicial review option, however, is one which was held to legitimise the appeal systems in relation to the ECHR (*R (on the application of Holding & Barnes plc) v Secretary of State for the Environment, Transport and the Regions* (2001)) and applied in Scotland in *County Properties Ltd v Scottish Ministers* (2001). This reasoning has been applied by the Scottish Government to the local review body procedures, as the potential for access to a court which is independent and impartial on judicial review type grounds is sufficient to cure any earlier difficulties with an administrative decision-making process (Poustie (2007) *JPL* 489 at 509). Notwithstanding that the question of ECHR and planning was laid to rest in the early years of the 21st century, the new Scottish system may yet result in a challenge under Art 6. This option is always open to users of the planning system, as is the right to resort to the European Court of Justice, if the appropriate pre-conditions have been satisfied.

MEDIATION

The White Paper *Modernising the Planning System* (2005) identified mediation as a tool that could be used within the planning process. More recently, the Scottish Government published "A Guide to the Use of Mediation in Planning System in Scotland" (2009). Informal negotiation and problem solving has always been part of the planning process. In the past it has been informal and relied on leadership by individual officers, councillors or professionals involved in the planning system. Mediation, however, is increasingly used in many areas of law to resolve disputes, and, therefore, it is appropriate to have it as part of the wider planning regime. The new system of LRBs and appeals is, in most cases, far less formal than the quasi-judicial process of the old planning appeal system and perhaps could be regarded as almost a form of mediation in itself. To date, however, those involved in the planning process are fully engaged with understanding and utilising the new statutory regime system of planning in Scotland. Once this is completely embedded, it may be that the mediation route will become more mainstream. Mediation certainly sits well within the culture change agenda of the new planning system in Scotland.

Essential Facts

Local Review

- Local developments will be dealt with mostly under delegated powers (1997 Act, s 43A). There are 3 months in which to submit a review of the decision to the local review bodies. The procedure is set out in the Town and Country Planning (Schemes of Delegation and Local Review Procedure) (Scotland) Regulations 2008 and Circular 7/2009: *Scheme of Delegation and Local Review.*
- Local review bodies consist of at least three elected councillors of the planning authority. Decisions must be made within 2 months and can be based on the existing information, written submissions or a hearing session.

Appeals

- Planning applications determined at planning or full committee of the local authority can be appealed to Scottish Ministers (1997 Act, s 47). This will mostly be major and national developments.
- Appeals must be brought within 3 months; are processed by the Directorate for Planning and Environmental Appeals and most are delegated to reporters. The procedure is set out in the Town and Country Planning (Appeals) (Scotland) Regulations 2008 and Circular 6/2009: *Planning Appeals.*
- Decisions on planning appeals can be made on existing information, written submissions, hearing sessions and inquiry sessions. The reporter decides the process to be followed.

Further challenge

- Further challenge of an appeal decision can be taken within 6 weeks of a decision (1997 Act, s 239) and by means of judicial review.

INDEX

NOTES

NOTES

NOTES

NOTES